NOW PLA
Learning Communication Through Film

2011 EDITION

Russell F. Proctor II
Northern Kentucky University

Darin Garard
Santa Barbara City College

Ronald B. Adler
Santa Barbara City College

New York   Oxford
Oxford University Press
2011

Oxford University Press, Inc., publishes works that further Oxford University's
objective of excellence in research, scholarship, and education.

Oxford   New York
Auckland   Cape Town   Dar es Salaam   Hong Kong   Karachi
Kuala Lumpur   Madrid   Melbourne   Mexico City   Nairobi
New Delhi   Shanghai   Taipei   Toronto

With offices in
Argentina   Austria   Brazil   Chile   Czech Republic   France   Greece
Guatemala   Hungary   Italy   Japan   Poland   Portugal   Singapore
South Korea   Switzerland   Thailand   Turkey   Ukraine   Vietnam

Copyright © 2011 by Oxford University Press, Inc.

Published by Oxford University Press, Inc.
198 Madison Avenue, New York, New York 10016
http://www.oup.com

Oxford is a registered trademark of Oxford University Press

ISBN 978-0-19-979380-8

Printing number: 9 8 7 6 5 4 3 2 1

Printed in the United States of America
on acid-free paper.

CONTENTS

INTRODUCTION

Communication is a human necessity—without it, we could scarcely coexist. Observing and analyzing communication patterns, interactions, and the many other intricacies of human contact is how we learn to project ourselves more effectively. Often times it is difficult to evaluate our own communication processes in an objective manner—but watching people communicating in films can be an excellent way to identify and understand many aspects of communication. Closely watching others engaged in communication on film can help bring theories and concepts to life.

This manual contains a section on **Feature Film Scenes**—a variety of specific scenes from a number of different films that illustrate the good, the bad, and the ugly of human interaction, along with discussion questions for each scene. A second section, **Full-Length Feature Films,** provides examples of entire films that provide insights into human communication, with a detailed synopsis of the movie along with discussion questions to prompt critical thinking.

Looking at the various characters in these films struggle with communication can be liberating as well as enlightening—we can observe it from a distance and, without being too self-conscious, pick up on both the good and the bad habits that can lead us to become better communicators. Have fun learning!

SECTION I
FEATURE FILM SCENES

Each of the entries in this section is a "stand alone" scene that illustrates communication concepts (with a strong focus on interpersonal communication). The scenes are listed below in alphabetical order; they are also arranged by category in the index at the end of the book. The time locations of the scenes are measured from the opening moment of the movie, just after the display of the film company (in other words, don't begin counting on your timer until all the previews on the video are finished).

Film: *Almost Famous*
Year: 2000
Central Concept: Self-Disclosure
Related Concepts: Identity Management, Group Communication
Approximate Scene Location: 96 minutes into the 122-minute movie
Approximate Scene Length: 4 minutes
Opening Line: Brief shot of plane flying through storm (no dialogue)
Closing Line: "Thank God we're all alive. We're going to make it!" (To capture facial expressions of the passengers after they realize they will survive, don't cut until scene ends, about 10 seconds after last line of dialogue.)

Scene Description: A 1970s rock band is on tour when its plane is caught in a violent storm. The prospect of imminent death moves several members of the group and its entourage to reveal facts and feelings they had previously kept to themselves. Some of the self-disclosing messages are positive; others are upsetting and disruptive. The scene offers a good foundation for exploring several dimensions of self-revelation: reasons for opening up, the conditions under which disclosure is likely to occur, and the risks and benefits of candor. (Note: the scene contains language that may offend some viewers.)

Discussion Questions:
1. Place the self-disclosures offered in this scene on a continuum, ranging from "appropriate under most conditions" to "inappropriate under most conditions." Describe the conditions under which the disclosures might be appropriate or inappropriate.
2. Which members of the group have been engaging in high levels of identity management with the others? What will happen to the management of their identities now that they've made these revelations?
3. Describe the following group communication concepts at work in this scene: ripple effect, conformity, openness, and boundaries.
4. Have you ever made a self-disclosure in a group of people that you later regretted? Discuss why you made the disclosure and how you managed your identity in later interactions with those people.

Film: *Click*
Year: 2006
Central Concept: Intercultural Incompetence
Related Concepts: Interpersonal Communication at Work, Coercive Power
Approximate Scene Location: 3 minutes into the 107-minute movie
Approximate Scene Length: 4 minutes
Opening Line: "Hmmm, well the interesting thing…"
Closing Line: "I'm just messing with you."

Scene Description: Workaholic architect Michael Newman is trying to earn a partnership in the firm headed by John Ammer. Ammer is arrogant, disrespectful, and insensitive in his interactions with clients and his employees, as evidenced by this scene. This scene could start a provocative discussion about intercultural and communicative competence, respect, and power in relationships.

Discussion Questions:
1. How do Ammer and Newman exhibit intercultural incompetence in their meeting with their Middle Eastern clients?
2. How could they enhance their intercultural competence?
3. Describe the dimensions of the workplace culture Ammer has created, evidenced by the exchanges between Ammer and Newman.
4. How does Ammer exercise coercive power in their relationship?

Film: *Clueless*
Year: 1995
Central Concept: Language
Related Concepts: Culture, Communication Competence, Public Speaking
Approximate Scene Location: 30 seconds into the 97-minute film
Approximate Scene Length: 4 minutes
Opening Line: "Did I show you the lumped-out jeep daddy got me?"
Closing Line: "If she doesn't do the assignment, I can't do mine."

Scene Description: Cher and her friends live in their own "contempo-casual" culture and speak their own language (depicted throughout this scene with words such as "jeepin," "outie," and "buggin'"). Their linguistic code gives them a sense of shared identity and excludes those who are not in their group. Near the end of the scene, Cher uses her group's jargon in a public speaking context, and her speech is not successful, demonstrating that language which is appropriate for an informal context is not appropriate for a formal one.

Discussion Questions:
1. Identify words/terms used by Cher and her friends that are unique to their culture. Which words/terms were not familiar to you?
2. Why do teenagers create new words and/or give old words new meanings?
3. Is it appropriate to use slang and jargon in public speeches?
4. Discuss this scene in terms of interpersonal, intercultural, and public speaking competence.

Film: *Dead Man Walking*
Year: 1996
Central Concept: Perception (Stereotyping and Prejudice)
Related Concepts: Communication Climate, Listening, Language
Approximate Scene Location: 40 minutes into the 120-minute film
Approximate Scene Length: 3 minutes
Opening Line: "Rain, rain, rain . . . that's a bad sign." (in the middle of a prison cell discussion)
Closing Line: "Can we talk about something else?"

Scene Description: This scene is an interpersonal communication tour de force. Helen Prejean is a nun who befriends death-row prisoner Matthew Poncelet prior to his execution. She confronts Poncelet about his prejudices regarding African-Americans. Poncelet's perceptions and language are filled with stereotypes and generalizations about "niggers" and "coloreds." Prejean's questions and responses require him to think (which he doesn't seem to want to do) about inaccuracies in his generalizations. Some of her comments are loaded and get defensive reactions; most are reflective and allow Poncelet to hear his prejudices in another voice. When Prejean's probing digs too deep (she gets him to realize "it's lazy people you don't like," not blacks), Poncelet asks Prejean to change the subject—which she agrees to do. This scene is worthy of line-by-line analysis.

Discussion Questions:
1. What factors influenced Poncelet's perceptions, prejudices, and stereotypes?
2. What listening skills does Prejean use to draw information from Poncelet? How do these skills get/keep Poncelet talking and thinking?
3. What questions/statements by Prejean prompt a defensive response from Poncelet?
4. Discuss the use of responsible and irresponsible language in the scene and its relationship to communication climate.

Film: *Election*
Year: 1999
Central Concept: Persuasion
Related Concept: Public Speaking
Approximate Scene Location: 36 minutes into the 103-minute film
Approximate Scene Length: 5 minutes
Opening Line: "We'll move on now to the presidential race."
Closing Line: "Don't vote at all!"

Scene Description: Three candidates are running for student government president at Carver High School: Tracy, Paul, and Tammy. Each is required to give a brief speech at a student assembly. Tracy's presentation is memorized, well constructed, and delivered with precision and flair (and a dose of overconfidence, which generates crude catcalls from students who think she is stuck up). Paul, a popular athlete, reads his speech directly from his notecards. While his content is solid, he has little or no eye contact, facial expression, or vocal variety—and the students don't know how to respond (they are prompted to applaud by a teacher). Tammy, Paul's sister, thinks that student government is a joke; she is running for election to spite her brother and his girlfriend. She speaks extemporaneously and with passion about the "pathetic" election process and encourages people to either vote for her or not vote at all. She gets a rousing response.

Discussion Questions:
1. Identify the strengths and weaknesses of each of the candidates' speeches.
2. Evaluate the persuasive appeals of each candidate in terms of logos, pathos, and ethos.
3. Which candidate would get your vote—and why?

Film: *Fantastic Mr. Fox*
Year: 2009
Central Concept: Leadership
Related Concepts: Group Cohesiveness, Power in Groups
Approximate Scene Location: 58 minutes into the 87-minute film
Approximate Scene Length: 3 minutes
Opening Line: "My suicide mission has been canceled."
Closing Line: "I doubt they had opossums in ancient Rome."

Scene Description: *Fantastic Mr. Fox* is director Wes Craven's interpretation of the classic Roald Dahl novel, by the same name. Filmed in stop-motion animation, the plot revolves around the adventures of Mr. Fox, a wild fox stuck in the mundane routines of raising and supporting his family. Unable to contain his natural instincts, Fox steals food from the local farmers until he pushes them too far, and an all-out war on animals ensues. After their homes are destroyed and his nephew taken hostage, Fox has to find a way to save his family and friends from the farmers' wrath. In this scene, Fox needs to rally support for his new plan to stop the farmers and rescue his nephew. He resumes his toast to his companions, but this time Fox points out their strengths as individuals and as a team. Reminding them of their unique talents and skills, Fox successfully creates group cohesion and motivates his followers to support his plan.

Discussion Questions:
1. Which factors (e.g., shared goals, perceived threats, etc.) does Mr. Fox rely on to motivate his group followers and create cohesiveness? Identify and provide examples.
2. Identify which type (or types) of power in groups that Fox demonstrates. How effective would his style be in different small group contexts (e.g., a family conflict or business meeting)? Why?
3. Which theory of leadership effectiveness (Trait, Style, or Situational) best exemplifies Mr. Fox's approach? Explain your choice.
4. Pick one example from your life when you were a follower in a small group, such as a sports team, summer camp, or work group. How did your leader attempt to create group cohesiveness? What types of power did your leader exercise? Which leadership approach was taken?
5. Pick a different example from your life when you were the leader in a small group, again such as a sports team, summer camp, or work group. How did you attempt to create group cohesiveness? What types of power did you exercise? Which leadership approach did you take?

Film: *Finding Forrester*
Year: 2000
Central Concept: Perception (Stereotyping)
Related Concepts: Culture, Identity Management
Approximate Scene Location: 18 minutes into the 136-minute film
Approximate Scene Length: 1 minute
Opening Line: "I'm not going to do anything to your car, man."
Closing Line: "No problem, man"

Scene Description: Jamal is an African-American teenager whose intelligence earns him a full scholarship to a prestigious, all-white prep school. He lives, however, in a tough, all-black neighborhood—so he often feels caught between two cultures. In this scene, a white man parks a sporty BMW in Jamal's neighborhood. When Jamal approaches the car, he perceives the driver reacting defensively. The two men have a tense conversation in which Jamal, by demonstrating his knowledge about the BMW company, attempts to disprove any stereotypes the driver might have about him.

Discussion Questions:

1. Describe how and why both the driver and Jamal engage in stereotyping at the outset of this scene. What nonverbal and verbal cues are involved?
2. Explain the role of selection, organization, and interpretation in the perceptions these two men hold of each other. Do their perceptions change as a result of their conversation? If so, how and why?
3. Discuss how the driver and Jamal engage in identity management throughout this scene. Use three words to describe the identity that each man tries to present.

Film: *Ghost Town*
Year: 2008
Central Concept: Avoidance of Communication
Related Concepts: Unwillingness to Communicate, Listening, Self-Disclosure
Approximate Scene Location: 5 minutes into the 102-minute film
Approximate Scene Length: 2 minutes
Opening Line: "Okay, go ahead and spit."
Closing Line: "So cute"

Scene Description: Bertram Pincus would be happy if other people simply left him alone. Paraphrasing John Donne he proclaims "*This* man is an island." Although Bertram enjoys the comfortable routine of his job as a dentist, he cannot stand the scripted conversations with his patients and coworkers. To make his life even worse, a complication during a medical procedure leaves Bertram with an unusual ability: he can now communicate with dead people as well as the living. In this scene, Bertram displays his style of avoiding communication with others. It works well to illustrate both verbal and nonverbal cues of avoidance, which students should easily identify. Moreover, this scene will provide a springboard to students' personal examples of communication avoidance.

Discussion Questions:

1. Identify both verbal and nonverbal cues that illustrate how Bertram attempts to avoid communication with others.
2. Even though Bertram obviously hears other people, how could his style of communication be considered ineffective listening? Which type of ineffective listening is it? Please explain.
3. Consider your own personal experiences with trying to avoid communicating with others. What were the reasons you were unwilling to communicate? What cues (both verbal and nonverbal) did you exhibit to illustrate your unwillingness? How did the other person respond?
4. Although this scene is entirely face-to-face, how has technology (e.g., cell phones, computers, etc.) changed the ways we avoid communication with others? Is avoidance easier or more difficult now because of technology?

Film: *Grease*
Year: 1978
Central Concept: Identity Management
Related Concepts: Nonverbal, Communication Competence
Approximate Scene Location: 22 minutes into the 110-minute movie
Approximate Scene Length: 2 minutes
Opening Line: "Hey, Sandy, we've got a surprise for you."
Closing Line: "Sandy, men are rats."

Scene Description: Sandy and Danny spent the summer in a blissful romance (the subject of the hit song, "Summer Nights"). When they parted ways at the end of the season, they thought they would never see each other again. Sandy's family moves, however, she ends up attending Rydell High. When she tells her new friends about her summer fling with a guy named Danny, they figure out that it's the same Danny who attends Rydell—and they set them up for a surprise "re-meeting." When Danny and Sandy first see each other, their faces and voices fill with delight. Quickly, however, Danny realizes he is in front of his hood buddies—and he changes his persona to be tough and cool rather than sensitive and sweet. Sandy is bewildered and devastated that the Danny she knew over the summer is so dramatically different from the Danny at Rydell High.

Discussion Questions:
1. Discuss this scene in terms of identity management. Why does Danny's self-presentation change so dramatically, while Sandy's does not?
2. Discuss the nonverbal messages Danny sends in this scene. When and how does he (and doesn't he) "leak" information about how he really feels?
3. Would you assess Danny as being "phony" or "communicatively competent" in this scene? What is the line of difference between the two? Explain your answer with concepts from the textbook.
4. Have you ever been in a similar situation where you felt "caught" between people you know from very different roles and contexts? How did you handle it?

Film: *Gung Ho*
Year: 1986
Central Concept: Culture
Related Concept: Communication Competence, Public Speaking
Approximate Scene Location: 8 minutes into the 110-minute film
Approximate Scene Length: 4 minutes
Opening Line: "Hi, fellas" (after entering the building with screen in hand)
Closing Line: "C'mon . . . c'mon" (with head in hands)

Scene Description: A scene reminiscent of *The Ugly American*: Hunt Stevenson goes to Japan in an attempt to lure Assan Motors to bring their business to his hometown of Hadleyville. His pitch to the Assan executives is an excellent example of what *not* to do. Clearly, Stevenson has not analyzed his audience or the setting (e.g., he lugs a projector screen to the session, not realizing that the room in which he is presenting is very high-tech). Moreover, he makes comments that are culturally insensitive (e.g., references to World War II) and interpersonally offensive (e.g., coarse references to women and underwear). The scene is very funny, but it is also uncomfortable.

Discussion Questions:
1. In what ways does Hunt Stevenson exhibit intercultural incompetence?
2. In what ways does Stevenson demonstrate that he has not analyzed his audience/setting?
3. How could Stevenson have made this pitch more effectively?

Film: *He's Just Not That Into You*
Year: 2009
Central Concept: Technology
Related Concepts: Computer-Mediated Communication, Relational Stages, Relational Maintenance
Approximate Scene Location: 67 minutes into the 129-minute film
Approximate Scene Length: 2 minutes
Opening Line: "He's leaving his wife for me!"
Closing Line: "Yeah…I felt like we connected."

Scene Description: Inspired by a pop culture book with the same name, *He's Just Not That Into You* dispenses romantic advice to its hopelessly confused female cast. Stacked with stereotypes, the entire film is intended to be a lesson on reading subtle verbal and nonverbal cues of potential romantic partners – to determine if he really is "into you." In this scene, Mary is expressing her frustration with today's technologically-driven dating culture. Exasperated, Mary tells her girlfriend Anna how she longs for simpler times when technology was less ubiquitous and dating was a face-to-face experience.

Discussion Questions:
1. Explain why Mary is so upset. Does she have a legitimate complaint? Why or why not?
2. Identify the types of technologies (e.g., email, cell phones, social networking sites) you utilize to *initiate* romantic relationships. Which medium is the most effective? Why? Which mediums are more effective for *maintaining* romantic relationships?
3. Describe a personal example when you experienced *benefits* from using technology instead of face-to-face communication. What is gained by using these technologies?
4. Likewise, describe a personal example when you felt *restricted* by using technology instead of face-to-face communication. What is lost by using these technologies?

Film: *Hitch*
Year: 2005
Central Concept: Interpersonal Relationships
Related Concepts: Nonverbal, Gender Influence on Relationships
Approximate Scene Location: 43 minutes into the 118-minute movie
Approximate Scene Length: 9 minutes
Opening Line: "Keep it simple, like we practiced."
Closing Line: "When they're good"

Scene Description: In *Hitch*, Alex "Hitch" Hitchens is a New York date doctor who teaches men how to romance the women of their dreams. Hitch's latest client is Albert Brennaman, a nerdy financial consultant who needs to develop a more macho communication style to win the heart of wealthy and beautiful Allegra Cole. The scene provides many examples of incompetent interactions and dating behaviors to discuss.

Discussion Questions:
1. How, specifically, does Hitch encourage Albert to change his verbal communication when interacting with Allegra?
2. Which nonverbal behaviors does Hitch coach Albert to change, and why?
3. What bits of advice does Hitch offer Albert to increase his attractiveness? Which tips do you believe are and are not sound?

Film: *I Love You, Man*
Year: 2009
Central Concept: Terminating Relationships
Related Concepts: Conflict, Friendship Rules, Relational Maintenance
Approximate Scene Location: 82 minutes into the 105-minute film
Approximate Scene Length: 3 minutes
Opening Line: "Yeah…it's open"
Closing Line: "Bye, Anwar."

Scene Description: As the title may suggest, *I Love You, Man* focuses on the male friendship – or "bromance" – between Peter and Sydney. Peter is a newly engaged realtor living in Los Angeles. When his fiancée asks him who his best man will be at their wedding, Peter suddenly realizes that he does not have any male friends. At a chance encounter during a house showing, Peter meets Sydney, a free-spirited individual also looking for friendship. The remainder of the film follows the stages of Peter and Sydney's relationship, complete with escalating, bonding, and deteriorating. In this scene, Peter confronts Sydney about several recent billboards around Los Angeles baring his likeness. Conflict ensues, Peter and Sydney 'break-up' and end their friendship. The scene works as an effective illustration of Knapp's terminating stage, along with how individuals establish and violate friendship rules.

Discussion Questions:
1. Explain how this scene demonstrates Knapp's terminating stage of relational deterioration.
2. Are there certain 'rules' to follow when ending friendships? Identify three rules you follow.
3. Are there certain 'rules' to follow for ending romantic relationships? Identify three rules you follow.
4. Describe a personal example when you ended a friendship. Was the termination a gradual withdrawal from your friend, or was it a sudden ending of the relationship?
5. In order to avoid reaching the terminating stage, what are strategies you use to maintain a friendship? Identify three relational maintenance strategies you use to keep your friendships from terminating.

Film: *The Invention of Lying*
Year: 2009
Central Concept: Self-Disclosure
Related Concepts: Honesty, Uncertainty Reduction, Identity Management, Saving Face
Approximate Scene Location: 4 minutes into the 99-minute film
Approximate Scene Length: 3 minutes
Opening Line: "This is not as nice as I remember it."
Closing Line: "How is your mom? Alright? Great!"

Scene Description: *The Invention of Lying* is a fictional tale about a world where no one can lie, not even a fib or a white lie – except one man. Mark Bellison discovers his unique gift and sets out to solve all of the world's problems, become rich and famous, and win the heart of the woman he loves. Predictably, Mark's plans do not always turn out the way he envisioned them. Perhaps the film would be more aptly titled *Too Much Self-Disclosure*, since the storyline really isn't so much about lying. Instead, it's more about the inability to refrain from verbalizing your every thought. The characters say whatever pops into their heads, no matter the context, and apparently without any negative outcomes – indeed a fictional tale. In this scene, Mark is on a date with Anna McDoogles. It is a typical first-date scenario for both characters, complete with feelings of uncertainty and anxiety about each other. Well, it's typical except for one small detail: they cannot control their self-disclosure. Pay special attention to the topics that are discussed, along with their atypical answers. In a world where honesty isn't simply the best policy – it's the only policy – a little self-disclosure can go a very long way.

Discussion Questions:
1. Using the terms depth, breadth, and reciprocity of self-disclosure, how is their first date typical of most first dates? How is it different from most first dates?
2. Consider your own past experiences on first dates. What topics do you typically discuss? Are these topics goal-oriented (e.g., to reduce uncertainty, to secure a second date, etc.)? In what ways?
3. Compare and contrast the characters' public and private selves. How are they managing their identity through communication?
4. Describe a situation when you were aware of your different selves, and you felt the need to manage your identity. Were you successful?
5. Is honesty always the best policy? Describe a situation when saving someone's face, without being completely honest, was the best choice – the choice of a competent communicator.

Film: *Invictus*
Year: 2009
Central Concept: Persuasive Speaking
Related Concepts: Credibility, Audience Analysis, Leadership and Power
Approximate Scene Location: 27 minutes into the 134-minute film
Approximate Scene Length: 8 minutes
Opening Line: "And now for the next item on our agenda."
Closing Line: "A luxury. We only needed one more yes than no."

Scene Description: *Invictus* is the real-life story about then South African President Nelson Mandela, and his plan to use rugby to unite his country following the demise of apartheid. Set in 1994-1995, newly elected President Mandela is struggling to move his nation forward, both politically and economically, in the eyes of the world. While attending a rugby match of the Springboks, the country's national rugby team, Mandela notices that blacks actually cheer against their home team – for them a longstanding symbol of racism and hatred – while Afrikaners (whites) root for the Springboks. Knowing that South Africa would host the Rugby World Cup in one year, Mandela enlists the aid of the Springbok's captain to promote the sport as a symbol of unity and nationalism, instead of hatred and violence. In this scene, Mandela must persuade South Africa's National Sports Council (the governing body in charge of the country's sports) not to change the Springbok team's name and colors. The National Sports Council, like most of the country's black citizens, views the Springboks as a symbol of apartheid. Learning that the Council has voted to dismantle the Springboks, Mandela rushes to their meeting in an attempt to persuade them otherwise. Facing a hostile audience, Mandela uses his credibility and audience analysis to successfully, by a narrow margin, convince the Council of his viewpoint.

Discussion Questions:
1. Using propositions, outcomes, and directness, identify the type of persuasive speech Mandela gives.
2. How does Mandela adapt to his audience (the National Sports Council)? What strategies does he use to appeal to this target audience?
3. Recall a time when you gave a speech to persuade, even an informal talk to a group. What strategies did you use to adapt to your audience? Were you successful? If not, how could you have increased your success through improved audience analysis?
4. Consider Mandela's credibility as a speaker. What characteristics about him increase the audience's perception of his credibility? How does Mandela use these characteristics in his speech?
5. Think back to a moment when you were in the audience for a persuasive speech. Did you consider the speaker to be credible? Why? If not, what could the speaker have done to increase your perceptions of his or her credibility?
6. Identify the types of power Mandela uses to influence the National Sports Council. How are power and credibility necessarily interwoven? Is it possible to separate them?

Film: *The Joy Luck Club*
Year: 1993
Central Concept: Culture
Related Concept: Communication Competence
Approximate Scene Location: 43 minutes into the 138-minute film
Approximate Scene Length: 4 minutes
Opening Line: "The next week I brought Rich to Mom's birthday dinner" (Waverly's voice)
Closing Line: "All this needs is a little soy sauce"

Scene Description: Waverly, a Chinese-American woman, brings her Anglo-American boyfriend Rich home for a dinner cooked by her Chinese mother, Lindo. Rich unknowingly insults Waverly's family when he fails to follow the rules of Chinese dining. For instance, he shocks everyone at the table by taking a large first serving of the entree. As Waverly explains in her narration, it is customary in Chinese culture to take only a small spoonful of a dish until everyone else has had some. Rich's biggest mistake is when he misunderstands Lindo's description of her prized entree. Lindo says, "This dish no good. Too salty." Rich decodes the message literally, not paying attention to Lindo's nonverbal cues. The family knows that when Lindo insults her cooking, it means she is pleased with it. The implicit rule is to eat some, then compliment it profusely. Instead, Rich floods the prized dish with soy sauce and assures Lindo that it is not beyond repair.

Discussion Questions:
1. What differences between American and Chinese cultures are depicted in this scene? Use terms from lecture and text in your analysis.
2. What could Rich have done to enhance his intercultural competence?

Film: *License to Wed*
Year: 2007
Central Concept: Listening
Related Concepts: Empathic Listening, Social Support Messages, Listening and Gender
Approximate Scene Location: 71 minutes into the 91-minute film
Approximate Scene Length: 2 minutes
Opening Line: "It wasn't supposed to be like this."
Closing Line: "I don't need anyone telling me!"

Scene Description: Ben Murphy and Sadie Jones are head-over-heels in love with each other. Ben proposes to Sadie, she accepts, and the happy couple begins planning their wedding. In order to be married at the church of Sadie's dreams, however, they learn that they must participate in a prenuptial course taught by the eccentric Reverend Frank. The Reverend's intense, and intrusive, course creates conflict between Ben and Sadie, resulting in their break-up and cancellation of the wedding. In this scene Ben is talking to his best friend, Joel, seeking his support and advice about how to get Sadie back. Unfortunately for Ben, Joel is an incompetent listener. In an otherwise forgettable film, this scene illustrates well how most typical forms of social support are ineffective.

Discussion Questions:
1. How would you label and describe Joel's style of listening? Use examples from their dialogue to justify your answer.
2. Clearly Joel's listening style is not working for Ben. What could Joel have said to Ben that would have been more competent? Create and role-play a new dialogue between Ben and Joel that incorporates your suggestions.
3. This scene supports the gender stereotype that men tend to respond to others' problems by giving advice. What has been your experience with listening style differences because of gender?
4. Recall a recent episode when you were seeking social support from someone. Describe what was said during the conversation and your perception of the outcome, whether it was positive or negative.

Film: *Love Actually*
Year: 2003
Central Concepts: Nonverbal (Deception and Leakage)
Related Concepts: Ethics of Deception
Approximate Scene Location: 28 minutes into the 135-minute film
Approximate Scene Length: 1 minute, 30 seconds
Opening Line: "So, what's the problem?"
Closing Line: "You're right. Total agony"

Scene Description: Daniel is very worried about his 11-year-old stepson, Sam. Sam's mother died recently, and he has spent nearly all his time alone in his room, leading Daniel to wonder if Sam is using drugs. In this scene, Daniel learns that Sam's "problem" is that he is in love. Daniel is delighted that drugs are not the issue, but he quickly realizes that Sam is taking this puppy love very seriously—and as a result, Daniel attempts to mask the relief and elation he is feeling.

Discussion Questions:
1. Daniel is trying to hide his happiness from Sam, but he is having a hard time doing it. What indications of leakage (showing his true feelings) do you see in Daniel?
2. Why do you think Daniel feels the need to hide his feelings of joy from Sam?
3. Daniel is trying to lie about his feelings. Do you think it's wrong for Daniel to deceive Sam in this manner? Explain your answer.

Film: *Mean Girls*
Year: 2004
Central Concept: Communication Climate
Related Concepts: Conflict, Empathy
Approximate Scene Location: 70 minutes into the 96-minute film
Approximate Scene Length: 5 minutes, 30 seconds
Opening Line: "Ms. Norbury, you're a successful, caring, intelligent, graceful young woman."
Closing Line: "Suck on that. Aye yie yie yie!" (as she falls backward to be caught by the other girls)

Scene Description: The girls of the junior class at North Shore High School are constantly in conflict. The disagreements, disconfirmation, and backstabbing (including mean evaluations written in a scrapbook called a "Burn Book") reach a breaking point when the fighting nearly leads to a riot. In response, the school principal calls all the junior girls to the gym where one of the school's teachers, Ms. Norbury, leads them in an "attitude makeover."

Discussion Questions:
1. What is Ms. Norbury's purpose with the two exercises she does where the girls close their eyes? How does it enhance the communication climate and empathy level among the girls?
2. Ms. Norbury says, "You all have got to stop calling each other sluts and whores. It just makes it okay for guys to call you sluts and whores." Do you agree with her assessment? Discuss in terms of course concepts.
3. What style(s) of conflict management does Ms. Norbury use? Is the approach effective in this situation? Discuss how well this approach would (or wouldn't) work in other conflict situations.

Film: *Medicine for Melancholy*
Year: 2009
Central Concept: Self-Concept
Related Concepts: Perception, Culture, Stereotyping
Approximate Scene Location: 64 minutes into the 88-minute film
Approximate Scene Length: 5 minutes
Opening Line: "A lot of second-hand smoke"
Closing Line: "I don't wanna talk anymore."

Scene Description: Understated yet thought provoking, *Medicine for Melancholy* is a slice-of-life story. Set in San Francisco, the film follows the awkward and uncertain moments of two twenty-somethings (Micah and Jo) after their one night stand. Not only do the characters struggle with defining their relationship, they each wrestle with definitions of their identity. In this scene, Micah and Jo are debating the meaning of being African-American while living in predominately-white San Francisco. Rather pointedly, Micah defines himself as "a black man," while Jo sees herself as more than any one quality. The scene encourages us to contemplate our own identity and worldview, and to question how we see ourselves through the eyes of others.

Discussion Questions:
1. When meeting someone for the first time (face-to-face), what do you typically notice about the other person? What judgments do you make? How does your perception, then, influence your communication with this person?
2. Describe how Micah sees himself, and how Jo sees herself. Speculate how and why each person formed their own worldviews.
3. Take a few minutes and write down ten different characteristics of your self-concept – who you think you are. After you have completed your list, explain how and why you define yourself this way. What experiences shaped your self-concept?
4. Do you think it is possible to define yourself by one quality (e.g., race or gender or class)? Describe a moment from your life when someone else defined you by only one quality, and treated you in a way that fulfilled that stereotype.

Film: *Nothing Like the Holidays*
Year: 2008
Central Concept: Family Communication
Related Concepts: Punctuation, Conflict, Identity Management
Approximate Scene Location: 47 minutes into the 98-minute film
Approximate Scene Length: 5 minutes
Opening Line: "Hey Father Torres, good to see you."
Closing Line: "Jesse!"

Scene Description: A Puerto Rican family with a long history in their Chicago neighborhood gathers for their annual Christmas get-together. Normally, the Rodriguez family participates in traditional rituals signifying the season – going to church, caroling, and parades. The siblings, however, soon realize that all is not well between their parents, and this holiday may be their last together as a family. In this scene, the eldest son (Mauricio) has taken it upon himself to organize a family intervention, hoping to prevent his parent's divorce. To her surprise, Anna (the family matriarch) comes home to find her three children, husband, and Father Torres sitting around the dinner table. The scene works well to illustrate family dynamics, as the discussion quickly shifts from the parents' divorce to the siblings' perceptions of their family roles.

Discussion Questions:
1. How would you describe this family system? What are the roles each family member plays? Are they symmetrical or complementary to each other?
2. Consider your own family system for a moment. What roles do you and other family members play? Would you consider your relationship with other members to be symmetrical or complementary?
3. Each member of the Rodriguez family appears to be talking from their own perspective, not the perspective of others. Choose two characters and explain their conflict by identifying differences in punctuation.
4. How does the mother manage her identity around Father Torres? Compare her perceived self with her presenting self.

Film: *Office Space* (Scene 1)
Year: 1999
Central Concept: Communication Climate
Related Concepts: Listening, Emotions, Nonverbal
Approximate Scene Location: 3 minutes into the 88-minute film
Approximate Scene Length: 5 minutes
Opening Line: Peter walking through the office door as the film credits roll
Closing Line: "Yes, I have the memo!"

Scene Description: From the minute Peter walks in the office on Monday morning at Initech, it is clear that he hates his mundane, dehumanizing job. One of the reasons is the way he is treated by his boss, Lumbergh, who approaches him and asks, "What's happening?" It is a counterfeit question because Lumbergh really doesn't want to know how Peter is doing, nor is he looking for any small talk about the weekend. Instead, he wants to confront Peter about a small mistake in his TPS report. He delivers a patronizing monologue to Peter in a calm, syrupy tone of voice—and shows no interest in Peter's explanation of the problem. After Lumbergh walks away, two other managers confront Peter about the same problem, using the same patronizing tone and lack of listening skills.

Discussion Questions:
1. Describe the communication climate between Peter and his managers. What factors from Gibb's climate model are evident in their interactions?
2. Discuss the managers' listening responses, both verbal and nonverbal, using terms from your textbook.
3. The managers in this scene use calm voices and avoid angry words, yet Peter still feels like he is being "yelled at." Explain how and why this is the case. How might the bosses have communicated their messages more effectively?
4. Watch this scene with the volume turned off. Attempt to describe what the characters are thinking and feeling simply by monitoring their nonverbal cues.

Film: *Office Space* (Scene 2)
Year: 1999
Central Concept: Communication Climate
Related Concepts: Language, Listening, Perception
Approximate Scene Location: 37 minutes into the 88-minute film
Approximate Scene Length: 1 minute
Opening Line: "Joanna, can I talk to you for a minute?"
Closing Line: "Some people choose to wear more; you do want to express yourself, don't you?"

Scene Description: Joanna is a waitress at Chotchkie's, a restaurant in the mold of Friday's and Bennigan's. Her manager is less than happy with her performance and calls her aside for a pep talk. Unfortunately, he creates a defensive communication climate by sending messages that are, to use Gibb's terms, evaluative, controlling, strategic, neutral, and superior. The manager is ambiguous and indirect as he talks to Joanna about her "flair" (a euphemism meant to describe the environment of fun at Chotchkie's, but something he measures by the number of buttons on her uniform). He also sends her negative nonverbal messages through a patronizing tone of voice and by rolling his eyes. Instead of describing what he wants from her, he asks impersonal and counterfeit questions such as, "What do you think of a person that only does the bare minimum?" and "Some people choose to wear more [flair buttons]; you do want to express yourself, don't you?"

Discussion Questions:
1. What is the communication climate between Joanna and her manager? What verbal and nonverbal messages are factors in the creating that climate?
2. Give examples of how the manager's language illustrates the concepts of vagueness, abstraction, and euphemisms. Describe how he could convey his concerns more precisely, concretely, and constructively.
3. Discuss how the manager uses counterfeit questioning in his listening responses. How could he have asked the same questions more sincerely?
4. Joanna attempts to use perception checking to clarify her manager's request. What effect does this have on their communication, and why?

Film: *One True Thing*
Year: 1998
Central Concept: Family Communication
Related Concept: Communication Climate
Approximate Scene Location: 29 minutes into the 127-minute film
Approximate Scene Length: 2 minutes, 30 seconds
Opening Line: "I'm glad you're home."
Closing Line: "Thanks for taking care of this."

Scene Description: Freelance writer Ellen Gulden grew up idolizing her father George, a self-important professor and literary critic. Ellen comes home for a surprise birthday party honoring George and soon learns that her mother is stricken with cancer. This scene takes place in George's study, where he invites Ellen to write the introduction to a volume of his collected essays. At first she is deeply honored by what she takes as a measure of her father's respect for her professional talent. But immediately after flattering Ellen with his offer, George dashes her spirits by heaping her arms full of soiled shirts and tossing off instructions on how to launder them.

Discussion Questions:
1. Describe the insights this scene offers into this family's system of operation. What seem to be the typical roles and relationships of the father, daughter, and (non-pictured) mother? How do the family members handle changes in the system?
2. Discuss the climate and the messages in this scene in terms of the following pairs of concepts: content/relationship; confirming/disconfirming; verbal/nonverbal; equality/superiority.

Film: *Pretty Woman*
Year: 1990
Central Concept: Self-Concept
Approximate Scene Location: 60 minutes into the 119-minute film
Approximate Scene Length: 2 minutes
Opening Line: "The first guy I ever loved was a total nothing . . ."
Closing Line: "You ever notice that?"

Scene Description: In this scene, Vivian shares her story with Edward of how she became a call girl. Her history with men, previous jobs, and prostitution suggests that she has low self-esteem and has molded her self-concept from the negative appraisals of others. Even when Edward tells Vivian that she has potential, she says, "People put you down enough times, you start to believe it." The experiences of her life make it difficult for Vivian to see herself as worthwhile.

Discussion Questions:
1. How is Vivian's self-concept related to reflected appraisal?
2. Why is it that "the bad stuff is easier to believe" when forming a self-concept?
3. How might Vivian's occupation play a role in forming and perpetuating her self-concept?

Film: *P.S. I Love You*
Year: 2007
Central Concept: Conflict
Related Concepts: Gender, Punctuation, Content and Relational Messages, Metacommunication, Relational Dialectics
Approximate Scene Location: Opening scene
Approximate Scene Length: 6 minutes
Opening Line: Holly and Gerry are shown walking up steps leaving the subway.
Closing Line: "Kiss mine…in English!"

Scene Description: Holly and Gerry are two young people passionately in love with each other. In fact, quite often their passion boils over into a heated argument. This scene begins with Gerry knowing that Holly is angry with him, but not knowing exactly why – her nonverbal communication speaks for itself. As he questions her about the source of this conflict, additional issues about their relationship start to seep out. Gerry becomes frustrated with Holly's insistence that what he says and what he means are two different things, and Holly is equally irritated with Gerry's cavalier approach to their relationship. The scene works on several levels, and mostly because it taps into many students' notions about romantic conflict.

Discussion Questions:
1. What styles of conflict do Holly and Gerry express in this scene? How might their gender differences influence these styles?
2. Holly and Gerry seem to have different perceptions of punctuation, when this conflict really started and by whom. How is Holly punctuating their argument? Gerry?
3. Explain how the scene illustrates the content and relational dimensions of messages, and identify examples of metacommunication.
4. Which dialectical tension is Holly experiencing, concerning her job and having a baby? How is she choosing to manage this tension? What is Gerry's response?
5. What could Holly and Gerry do to manage this conflict, and future ones, more competently?

Film: *The Pursuit of Happyness*
Year: 2006
Central Concept: Self-Fulfilling Prophecy
Related Concepts: Self-Actualization, Emotional Intelligence
Approximate Scene Location: 107 minutes into the 117-minute movie
Approximate Scene Length: 4 minutes
Opening Line: "Chris, thank you very much."
Closing Line: "Christopher, come here."

Scene Description: Struggling salesman Chris Gardner pursues a life-changing professional endeavor of becoming a stockbroker under the tremendous pressures of homelessness, tax seizure, jail time, and single parenthood. While caring for his son without any outside help, Gardner endures a grueling unpaid internship. He is determined to win employment in a program where only one of the twenty interns receives a job offer. In this powerful scene, Gardner interacts with his mentor at the end of his internship, when a hiring decision is being made by the company.

Discussion Questions:
1. Describe how Gardner communicates competently with his client and colleagues.
2. Apply the term "self-fulfilling prophecy" to Gardner's life story.
3. How does the final scene exemplify a moment of self-actualization for Gardner?
4. Given the extreme pressures placed on him, explain Gardner's apparent emotional intelligence.

Film: *The Remains of the Day*
Year: 1993
Central Concept: Nonverbal Communication
Related Concepts: Relational Intimacy, Relational Dialectics, Emotions
Approximate Scene Location: 87 minutes into the 135-minute film
Approximate Scene Length: 3 minutes
Opening Line: "Flowers" (Miss Kenton) "Hmm?" "Flowers."
Closing Line: "I really must ask you please not to disturb the few moments I have to myself."

Scene Description: *The Remains of the Day* focuses on the 1930s working relationship between Stevens, a reserved head butler of a huge English mansion, and Miss Kenton, the mansion's outspoken housekeeper. Stevens has learned to repress his emotions, which becomes obvious when Kenton surprises him in his den as he is reading. She invades his personal time and space, especially as she inches nearer and nearer to him. Kenton and Stevens have developed romantic feelings for one another, but his inability to express his emotions makes this situation uncomfortable, even painful, for the two of them. Does Stevens want Kenton to leave him alone, as his words command, or does he wish her to spend this quiet moment with him, as his eyes suggest? The contradiction between Stevens' verbal and nonverbal communication points to the dialectical tension of intimacy/distance in their relationship.

Discussion Questions:
1. Discuss the nonverbal messages being exchanged in this scene, using terms from this course.
2. Discuss the mixed messages in this scene. How and when do the content messages contradict the relationship messages?
3. What dialectical tensions are in evidence between Stevens and Kenton?
4. How did you feel as you watched this scene? Identify three specific emotions.

Film: *Sex Drive*
Year: 2008
Central Concept: Identity Management
Related Concepts: Computer-Mediated Communication, Self-Disclosure, Saving Face

Scene 1
Approximate Scene Location: Opening scene
Approximate Scene Length: 1 minute, 40 seconds
Opening Line: "We open up against Michigan in 2 weeks."
Closing Line: "I gotta bounce."

Scene 2
Approximate Scene Location: 16 minutes into the 109-minute film
Approximate Scene Length: 2 minutes
Opening Line: "What are you doing in there man?"
Closing Line: "Harsh!"

Scene(s) Description: Fueled by adolescent-themed humor, *Sex Drive* is a film fitting of the teen-angst and road trip genres. Although the film will not appear on any critics' top ten list, two scenes illustrate the process of identity management well.

Scene 1 – Ian is shown typing away on his laptop having a mediated conversation with a woman – except Ian's online identity does not match his face-to-face persona. Utilizing principles of selective self-presentation, Ian has created his ideal self online: a football player, physically attractive, and a smooth talker. (Note that some audiences may find the language in this scene to be inappropriate.)

Scene 2 is a face-to-face conversation, so Ian doesn't have the luxury of editing his words or misrepresenting his physical image. The real Ian is average looking, has difficulty talking with women, and works at a donut shop where he wears a ridiculous uniform. Here Ian misreads the cues of his female platonic friend, Felicia, and her disclosure of a new crush. Wanting to believe that Felicia has fallen for him, Ian mistakenly moves in for a romantic kiss. Watching how both parties attempt to save face during this embarrassing moment is both humorous and painful.

Separately, each scene could be utilized to demonstrate different forms of identity management. Taken together, both scenes provide a descriptive contrast between mediated and face-to-face self-presentation.

Discussion Questions:
1. Describe how Ian manages his identity online. What strategies of selective self-presentation does he use? What strategies do you use to manage your online identity?
2. Thinking about the concepts perceived self and presenting self, which one is Ian's online self? His face-to-face self? Speculate why he has difficulty aligning the two selves.
3. In the second scene, what strategies do Ian and Felicia use to save face during their awkward conversation?
4. Reflect on and describe an awkward conversation you had that was similar to Ian's. How did you manage the conversation? Were you able to save face? What did you learn from the experience?

Film: *Shark Tale*
Year: 2004
Central Concept: Identity and Impression Management
Related Concepts: Deception, Conflict Resolution
Approximate Scene Location: 75 minutes into the 90-minute movie
Approximate Scene Length: 4 minutes
Opening Line: "I am not a real sharkslayer."
Closing Line: "Sykes and Oscar's Whale Wash is open."

Scene Description: When the son of the shark mob boss is found dead, a small fish with attitude named Oscar is coincidentally found at the scene. Oscar takes the opportunity to toughen up his identity, posing as the "sharkslayer." Oscar soon learns that his deception and fake identity have ill effects on his life and relationships. The other main character, Lenny, is a great white shark and brother to the mob boss's son. Lenny has a sensitive side and a secret about his identity—he's a vegetarian shark who pretends to eat fish, but in reality is nauseated when forced to do so. In this scene, Oscar and Lenny admit to their deception and apologize to their relatives and friends.

Discussion Questions:
1. What were Oscar's and Lenny's reasons for telling lies about their identities?
2. Give a real-world example of presenting a false identity, and explain the likely reasons for this misrepresentation.
3. Describe the gendered expectations of Oscar and Lenny and why they lied to meet them.
4. Is misrepresenting one's identity ever ethical? Explain your answer, giving examples.

Film: *Shrek the Third*
Year: 2007
Central Concept: Self-Disclosure
Related Concepts: Linguistic Convergence, Reciprocity, Relational Development

Scene 1
Approximate Scene Location: 41 minutes into the 93-minute film
Approximate Scene Length: 2 minutes
Opening Line: "How humiliating"
Closing Line: "Help! I've been kidnapped by a monster trying to relate to me!"

Scene 2
Approximate Scene Location: 47 minutes into the 93-minute film
Approximate Scene Length: 2 minutes
Opening Line: "Look…Artie…um…"
Closing Line: "Yeah, I got that."

Scene(s) Description: For those viewers who saw the original *Shrek*, you'll likely remember Shrek's insightful analysis comparing ogres to onions – a scene practically written for social penetration theory. In *Shrek the Third*, viewers witness the ogre put his theory into action. Up to this point in the film, Shrek has had a difficult time building a relationship with young King Author (Artie) and convincing him to be the next king of Far, Far Away. In the first scene, Shrek exhibits incompetent communication: he yells at Artie, threatens to hit him with a club, and unconvincingly attempts to speak like a teenager. In the next scene, Shrek chooses to self-disclose intimate details about his own childhood and upbringing. Shrek gains Artie's trust, and their relationship progresses to another stage. (Note: A quick fast-forward is all that is necessary between the two scenes.)

Discussion Questions:
1. Describe how Shrek attempts linguistic convergence with Artie in scene 1. Why is Shrek unsuccessful? Can you think of a personal example of linguistic convergence, either as the sender or the receiver? Was it successful?
2. Apply principles of self-disclosure and explain how Shrek is able to gain Artie's trust in scene 2.
3. At the end of scene 2, which stage of relational development do you think Shrek and Artie have reached?

Film: *Superbad*
Year: 2007
Central Concept: Communication Competence
Related Concepts: Empathy, Cognitive Complexity, Language
Approximate Scene Location: 11 minutes into the 114-minute film
Approximate Scene Length: 1 minute
Opening Line: "Ms. Hayworth, I joined this class because I thought I would be cooking with a partner."
Closing Line: "Jules"

Scene Description: Seth and his best friend Evan are high school seniors desperately searching for one final party before graduation. Most of the time Seth's heart is in the right place, even if his foot is occasionally stuck in his mouth. In this scene, Seth attempts to explain to his Home Economics teacher the injustice of not having a cooking partner. During his argument, his language is sprinkled with vulgarity, and he insults his teacher's course, profession, and gender. While Seth does employ a few reasonable strategies to gain her compliance (qualifying his language, apologizing, and initiating subtle touch), his communication incompetence speaks for itself. (Warning: this scene contains some coarse language.)

Discussion Questions:
1. In what ways does Seth exhibit communication incompetence?
2. Consider the three dimensions of empathy. Describe Seth's success rate for each dimension.
3. Would you evaluate Seth as having high cognitive complexity? Why or why not?
4. Seth frequently uses the phrase "no offense" during his talk with Ms. Hayworth. What type of language device is this? Evaluate its effectiveness in this scene compared to your own use of this phrase.

Film: *Thank You for Smoking*
Year: 2006
Central Concept: Persuasion
Related Concepts: Ethos/Pathos/Logos, Social Judgment Theory, Fallacies of Reasoning, Ethics
Approximate Scene Location: 45 minutes into the 92-minute film
Approximate Scene Length: 5 minutes
Opening Line: "Pearl, we got company."
Closing Line: "No, Lorne. Either you keep all the money, or you give it all away."

Scene Description: Based on the novel by Christopher Buckley, this film is a satirical look at both the tobacco industry and the congressional lobbying system. Nick Naylor is the Vice President and lead spokesperson for the Academy of Tobacco Studies, an oxymoronic institution if there ever were one. Nick's job – at which he is quite successful – is to persuade whoever is listening that smoking cigarettes is not unhealthy. The film illustrates a variety of fallacious and morally questionable persuasive strategies. In this scene, Nick has been dispatched by big tobacco to the home of the actor who portrayed the Marlboro Man in cigarette ads. Now he is dying of lung cancer, and Nick is there to bribe him to keep quiet. What ensues is a clever example of illogical reasoning and unethical persuasion.

Discussion Questions:
1. Provide examples of ethos, pathos, and logos appeals made by Nick in his conversation with the Marlboro Man.
2. Use social judgment theory to explain how Nick successfully persuades the Marlboro Man to take the bribe. Given his high ego-involvement, plot out the Marlboro Man's latitudes of acceptance, rejection, and non-commitment, and arrange Nick's arguments along that continuum.
3. Describe three fallacies of reasoning that Nick uses in his argument. Why did the Marlboro Man not see these fallacies? Which fallacies have you found to be used most often in real-world examples, based on your personal observations?
4. In Nick's own words, his job requires "a moral flexibility" that most people don't have; in other words it's unethical. Discuss additional, real-world examples of persuasion that you have found to be unethical.

Film: *The Visitor*
Year: 2007
Central Concept: Identity Management
Related Concepts: Self-Concept, Self-Disclosure, Johari Window
Approximate Scene Location: 81 minutes into the 104-minute film
Approximate Scene Length: 3 minutes
Opening Line: "You know…I think that show was really kind of scary."
Closing Line: "It's kind of exciting not to know."

Scene Description: In Director Thomas McCarthy's *The Visitor*, Walter Vale is an economics professor and widower who has lost his passion for teaching, and for living. Seemingly sleepwalking through life, Walter has an unexpected encounter with an illegal immigrant couple (Tarek and his girlfriend Zainab) who are wrongly living in his New York City apartment. Instead of throwing them out onto the street, Walter graciously allows them to stay. And despite their many differences, Walter and Tarek develop a close friendship. Desperation strikes, however, when Tarek is arrested and faces immediate deportation back to Syria. What follows is an agonizing and heart-wrenching battle fought by Walter to free his friend Tarek. In this scene Walter and Tarek's mother, Mouna, are having a night out – a Broadway show followed by dinner. In this intimate moment, Walter reveals parts of his identity that before he had kept secret from Mouna, and perhaps even from himself. Walter's self-disclosure leaves him vulnerable, and the audience wonders how Mouna will respond.

Discussion Questions:
1. How would you describe Walter's public self? What about his perceived self? As he puts it, why is Walter "pretending" to be someone he isn't? Explain why his, or any person's, multiple identities could be so dissimilar.
2. Consider your own public and private selves. Are they similar? Dissimilar? Why?
3. Walter's self-disclosure is risky and clearly leaves him vulnerable. Speculate what effect this disclosure will have on his relationship with Mouna.
4. Use the Johari Window model to illustrate Walter's self-disclosure to Mouna. Draw two boxes, one before the conversation with Mouna and one after, to explain the change in information known between the two characters. Be sure to label the four quadrants within each box as Open, Blind, Hidden, and Unknown.

Film: *Waking Life*
Year: 2001
Central Concept: Linear communication model
Related Concepts: Ogden and Richards' Triangle of Meaning, Sapir-Whorf Hypothesis, Language
Approximate Scene Location: 11 minutes into the 100-minute film
Approximate Scene Length: 3 minutes
Opening Line: "Creation seems to come out of imperfection."
Closing Line: "That feeling might be transient, but I think it's what we live for."

Scene Description: As he strives to discover if he is awake or asleep, or somewhere in between, Wiley Wiggins listens to discussions on the meaning of life, free will, politics, existentialism, and many others. In this clip, Wiley is listening to a woman ponder the origins, functions, and power of language. The scene is successful because it breathes life into a sometimes abstract discussion of textbook terms, and does so in a visual way that many students can appreciate. The entire film is a series of philosophical, dream-like conversations between the protagonist and the characters he meets; the film was shot in live-action with digital cameras, then animators overlaid their drawings on top of the live images, creating a surreal effect for the viewer. Incidentally, some of the film was shot on the campus of the University of Texas, Austin, and several of the characters are faculty at the university.

Discussion Questions:
1. How does this scene illustrate the linear communication model? How does it illustrate limitations of this model, compared to the transactional model?
2. Explain how the scene illustrates all three parts of the Triangle of Meaning model.
3. Do you agree that "words are dead, they're inert."? Why or why not? Give examples.
4. Thinking about the Sapir-Whorf Hypothesis and linguistic relativity, discuss situations when you have felt constrained by language and meanings.
5. When have you had moments of shared meaning, shared narratives, with someone else? In what ways we can increase our chances of achieving shared meaning with others?

SECTION II
FULL-LENGTH FEATURE FILMS

Each of the film entries in this section provides information in the following categories:

Film Data: Year, Director, Length, and Rating
Characters/Actors: Principal actors and roles in the film
Communication Concepts: Primary communication topics in the film (listed alphabetically)
Viewing Information: General background and potential warning information about the film
Synopsis: A brief summary of the film's plot and themes
Discussion Questions: Questions (and answers to the first two) linking the film to communication concepts

The following are a number of films that have human communication as a central theme. The discussion questions that follow the basic data about the film are the heart of this section. The questions posed are not the only ones that can or should be asked, nor are the answers given for the first two films the only "right" way to respond to the questions. In fact, you may argue with some of the analyses and interpretations. That's fine—any good discussion about movies should engender disagreement. The questions (and answers) are provided simply to offer an example of how to analyze the film and the communication that goes on within it.

(500) DAYS OF SUMMER

Film Data
Year: 2009
Director: Marc Webb
Length: 95 Minutes
Rated: PG-13

Characters/Actors
Tom Hansen: Joseph Gordon-Levitt
Summer Finn: Zooey Deschanel

Communication Concepts
Attachment Styles
Commitment
Nonverbal Miscommunication
Relational Development and Dialectics

Viewing Information
In an ominous tone, a voice utters the opening line of the film: "This is not a love story." Indeed, it is not. Tom Hansen is a shy, hopeless romantic who writes greeting card lines for a living. Seemingly out of nowhere, Summer Finn walks into his life, and Tom is smitten at first sight. One problem, though: Summer does not believe in romance. Tom pursues Summer anyway, and although they do become involved romantically, Tom learns several painful lessons about unrequited love. Remember, this is not a love story.

Synopsis
Tom Hansen thought he had found "the one." Like her seasonal namesake, Summer Finn blew into Tom's life unexpectedly, and he was a changed man – though perhaps not for the better. *(500) Days of Summer* opens with Tom severely depressed, mourning his break-up with Summer. In non-linear fashion, the rest of the film portrays Tom's reflections on their relationship leading up to, and after, their break-up. Along the way, we are treated to moments of misunderstood signals, ruminations on romance, and a conflict of commitment.

Discussion Questions

1. **Identify Tom and Summer's stages of relational development, including their coming together and coming apart stages. How are differences in commitment demonstrated in these stages? How do the characters experience and manage the predictability versus novelty dialectic?**

   Given the film's nonlinear presentation, it provides a unique way of viewing relationship stages. Arguably, relationships themselves are not linear, and they do not follow predictable stages of development and decline. On the other hand, the film presents a compelling case study that they are.

Coming Together Stages:
During Days 1-8, Tom and Summer go through the Initiating and Experimenting stages. They exchange small talk, learning about each other's interests and similarities, and thereby reducing uncertainty – typical moments in these stages. On Day 11 Tom's version of the relationship is moving rapidly, since he

talks as if he and Summer are soul mates with multiple commonalities. Instead, Summer labels their relationship as "friends" on Day 27, seemingly removing any chances of reaching the Intensifying stage.

On Day 31 that perception shifts dramatically when Summer kisses Tom in the copy room at work. Day 34 marks the Intensifying stage for both parties. While role-playing at Ikea, Summer again labels their relationship as "not serious." And although Tom agrees, they do have sex later that night – students might view this as a friends-with-benefits relationship. Days 45-95 signify the Integrating stage: Summer and Tom spend much time together, learning about each other and developing their own relationship rituals. When Summer invites Tom to her place, importantly not until Day 109, Tom believes they have reached the Bonding stage. There, Summer reveals a depth of self-disclosure Tom had yet to see, and a strong sense of commitment is apparent.

Coming Apart Stages:
The first sign of relational discord, and Differentiating, occurs on Day 259. Tom gets into a bar fight defending Summer. Afterwards, they have another conflict about the status of their relationship: Summer continues to label them as friends, while Tom believes they are more. Examples of Circumscribing and Stagnating take place at Ikea on Day 282. Instead of participating in their role-playing routine, Summer is noticeably silent and distant. Day 290 marks the Terminating stage, presented cleverly at the beginning of the film, when Summer desires to "stop seeing each other." Up until Day 402 when Tom sees Summer again, he is noticeably depressed and angry. Talking with Summer on the train, encourages Tom to believe that they are coming together again. And indeed there are moments of Experimenting and Intensifying for Tom, but they are not mutual. On Day 476, Summer sees Tom at their favorite park. There she explains how she realized that she has a desire for commitment, but not with Tom.

Regarding the Predictability versus Novelty Dialectic, Tom consistently desires more predictability in their relationship. Tom wants routines that couples share, and he wants commitment. Tom chooses Moderation to manage this dialectic, continually compromising his need for predictability with Summer's desire for novelty. Summer, on the other hand, is comfortable with uncertainty and a lack of commitment. Summer uses Denial to manage this dialectic, ignoring certainty and predictability, up until the moment that she terminates their romantic relationship.

2. **Use attachment styles theory to label Tom and Summer's perspectives on love and relationships, and identify examples of their attachment styles. Are their different attachment styles necessarily incompatible? Explain.**

Attachment styles theory by John Bowlby presumes that individuals learn about relationships by interacting with others. More specifically, as children we develop attachment styles based on interactions with our primary caregivers (e.g., parents). Bowlby identified four possible attachment styles, each a different combination of positive or negative views of the self versus others.

The secure attachment style has a positive view of self and others, characterized by confident and affectionate behavior. Secures are comfortable loving and being loved by others. Individuals with a fearful attachment style have both a negative view of self and others, and they exhibit strong insecurities about forming relationships. The dismissive style is a combination of positive views of self and negative views of others. Dismissives are reluctant to commit to others and tend to view relationships as unnecessary. Lastly, the anxious/ambivalent attachment style has a negative view of self with positive views of others. This style is characterized by inconsistent behavior: at times anxious/ambivalents have strong desires for closeness, while other moments involve denying other's affections.

Out with their coworkers at a karaoke bar (0:18:40), both Tom and Summer explain their philosophy about relationships. Tom, the idealist, argues that true love does exist. For Tom, relationship commitment is a healthy and natural outgrowth of being human. Summer, on the other hand, believes that true love is a myth. Her philosophy is that relationships are messy, she has never been in love before, and she should enjoy herself being free and independent.

Tom, it seems, might be labeled as having a combination of secure and fearful attachment. Regarding his secure style, Tom clearly has a positive view of others as lovable. Tom believes in the concept of true love, and he desires commitment with someone else. On the other hand, Tom does exhibit acute depression and insecurities during break-ups with Summer, and thus might also demonstrate the fearful style (Bowlby argued that individuals gravitate toward one style throughout their lifetime, although recent research suggests that combinations of styles are possible).

For Summer, a dismissive attachment is her preferred style. Although likable, and lovable, Summer perceives relationships as unnecessary – and she is not afraid to express that view. Her style shifts, however, toward the end of the film when she marries someone else after her own "love at first sight" moment. An argument could be made that Summer also, at times, shows an anxious/ambivalent style. There are moments when she desires closeness, though the majority of the time Summer demonstrates a need for distance.

If you are more interested in love styles and not attachment, then a discussion could easily revolve around that topic. We would likely label Tom as having an eros love style, while Summer is more of a ludic lover (both for reasons mentioned above).

3. **Locate moments when Tom has difficulty reading Summer's nonverbal cues. Does Tom have poor nonverbal decoding skills, or is Summer difficult to read? What are their content and relational level meanings?**

There are several humorous scenes that illustrate the ambiguity of nonverbal communication. In one scene (0:14:47) Tom explains to his friends why his potential relationship with Summer "is off." While riding the elevator to their floor, Tom casually asks about her weekend. Summer replies that it was "goood" (said in a drawn-out way), and Tom misreads her paralanguage to mean that she had sex all weekend.

Moments later, Tom explains that he tried to tell Summer that he is interested in her, but she did not pick up his (rather high-context) signals. For example, when Summer asks if Tom needs anything from the copy room, Tom replies slyly, "I think you know what I need." Meant with a blank stare, Tom hedges and follows up with "toner." Later, knowing that she likes the band The Smiths, Tom blares their music from his computer as Summer leaves the office – his ambiguous nonverbal style falls on deaf ears.

Much later in the film (beginning at 1:00:25), Tom and Summer have stopped seeing each other. By chance they find themselves on the same train to a mutual friend's wedding; Tom is still in mourning over their break-up while Summer appears to have moved on. Long moments of sustained eye contact, smiling, and close proximity while at the wedding, all signal to Tom that Summer is still interested in him romantically. And when Summer invites Tom to a party at her place, he truly believes they are "getting back together" – there is a clever scene comparing Tom's expectations with reality. His expectations come crashing down when Tom learns that she is engaged.

In sum, yes, Tom does have difficulty reading Summer's intentions through her nonverbal communication, and these examples point toward the ambiguous nature of nonverbal cues. Perhaps students might regard Summer's style, and Tom's inability to read her, as a gender difference – a discussion of that possibility could be worthwhile.

AMERICAN TEEN

Film Data
Year: 2008
Director: Nanette Burstein
Length: 95 Minutes
Rated: PG-13

Characters/Actors
Hannah Bailey: Herself
Colin Clemens: Himself
Megan Krizmanich: Herself
Mitch Reinholt: Himself
Jake Tusing: Himself

Communication Concepts
Computer-Mediated Communication
Family Systems
Public/Private Self and Identity Management
Self-Concept/Looking-Glass Self/Self-Fulfilling Prophecy
Stereotypes/Prototypes/Scripts

Viewing Information

Like its classic predecessors in the teen-angst genre (see *The Breakfast Club*, *Clueless*, and *Mean Girls*), *American Teen* portrays the archetypal high school student. Unlike those fictional films, however, this is a documentary – these are real students simply being themselves. As the characters struggle to find their identity, some dreams are fulfilled while others deferred. Whether or not you agree with the accuracy of these stereotypes, each character has a story worth telling.

Synopsis

It is their senior year of high school in small Warsaw, Indiana. What happens this year will have a strong influence on the future lives of five students. In this documentary we learn about the ups and downs of Hannah, Colin, Megan, Mitch, and Jake. Like a reality television show, the cameras follow the characters everywhere and document their most intimate moments. Will Hannah break free from this small-town life? Will Colin get the basketball scholarship he desires? And will Jake finally find true love? Each of these questions is answered in *American Teen*.

Discussion Questions

1. **The five main characters (Hannah, Colin, Megan, Mitch, and Jake) are prototypical American high school students, each representing a certain clique. What stereotype does each character fulfill? What scripts do the characters follow? Choose two of the five main characters and analyze their self-concept. Use the terms "looking-glass self" and "self-fulfilling prophecy" in your analysis.**

Hannah Bailey – Hannah fills the rebel stereotype. She readily admits that she does not fit in with her conservative community, and she cannot wait to leave Warsaw. She loves to draw, paint, and make art – anything that channels her creative energies. Hannah follows the script of the outsider. She is not part of any club or extracurricular activity, and more importantly she does not want to be. When Hannah starts dating fellow character Mitch, she is suddenly thrown into the popular crowd, with unfortunate but not surprising consequences. In one of the film's animated sequences, Hannah reveals her looking-glass self: she does not like who she is. Granted, at least part of her self-esteem may be biologically related to her mother's depression. Not fitting in at school, feeling like she is teased by her peers, living with her grandmother after practically being abandoned by her parents – each of these events also relates to Hannah's negative self-concept.

Colin Clemens – Colin portrays the jock of the film. Because of his athletic prowess on the basketball court, Colin navigates the popular crowd. Apparently high school basketball is everything in Warsaw, and Colin is treated like a hero. True to his script, Colin shoulders the emotional burden of every win – and loss. He also has the additional challenge of following in the footsteps of his father, himself a legendary figure in Warsaw basketball history and a darn good Elvis impersonator. Although popular, funny, and easygoing among his friends, we can see Colin's struggle to step outside his father's shadow and find his own identity.

Megan Krizmanich – Megan is the queen bee of Warsaw High School. Equally admired and hated by her peers, she is perhaps the most complicated and misunderstood character of the film. Megan follows the script of ultimate over-achiever: she gets good grades, belongs to all the right clubs, volunteers for school activities, and still finds time to party with the other popular kids. Under that glossy veneer, however, is a troubled young woman. When Megan was younger her older sister committed suicide in their house. The loss of her sister left a hole in the family system Megan felt forced to fill. She constantly seeks approval from her father, even as he sets her up to disappoint him. She acts out her frustrations and constant high expectations by drinking, vandalizing, and simply being obnoxious to her so-called friends. It is tempting to dislike Megan and cast her aside. Given a chance, however, she becomes one of the more sympathetic characters of the film.

Mitch Reinholt – Mitch is typecast as the heartthrob. He is the least documented character of the film. Handsome and athletic, Mitch's script is a more subdued Colin. He also might be the best example of an inaccurate looking-glass self. Mitch knows that others see him as popular and outgoing, but that's not really him. Only when he dates Hannah does the audience receive a peek into his true identity – shy, somewhat goofy, and someone longing to just be himself. Predictably, Mitch succumbs to the expectations of his peers and breaks up with Hannah, displaying a role he is unable to discard.

Jake Tusing – Jake portrays the geek of the film, and he does not miss a beat. He fulfills all the qualities of his stereotype: he is in the band, loves to play video games, and has few friends. Socially awkward to the point of incompetence, Jake struggles forming relationships with others. Like his fellow character Hannah, he too follows the outsider script. Unlike Hannah, though, Jake longs for companionship with others. For Jake, having a girlfriend is his ultimate goal. Unfortunately for him, real relationships are not formed as easily, or heroically, as a character in one of his video games. Jake also represents the best example of self-fulfilling prophecy. During his animation scene, he reveals that an unfortunate incident in middle school gave him the geek label and made him "be so afraid" of who he is.

2. **One benefit of watching a documentary is that the viewer is allowed to hear what the characters really think, then to watch how those thoughts and feelings are translated into action. How do their characters' private selves compare to their public versions? How do the characters manage their identity in different contexts? Provide examples.**

Mitch provides a good starting point to examine public and private selves. Among his friends, Mitch is the handsome heartthrob. Quick with a smile or a joke, Mitch appears to glide easily through high school. When he dates Hannah, however, his private self becomes more pronounced. Alone with Hannah, Mitch displays his shy, almost nerdy self. In a voice-over he reveals his true feelings for her – he likes hanging out with Hannah. At a party among his peers, however, Mitch's public image and potential loss of face dating Hannah become more important and he suddenly stops seeing her.

Megan also represents a good example of the public/private self dichotomy. To everyone except her closest friends and family, Megan appears to have it all: attractiveness, wealth, and plenty of friends. Privately, though, Megan feels enormous pressure to live up to her family's expectations. For example, rather than lose face and disclose the source of her anger (the anniversary of her sister's suicide) to her best female friend, Megan becomes confrontational and doesn't speak to her friend for a week. In another scene, a decision by the Homecoming Council sparks Megan to channel her frustrations into vandalism. She also has a confusing relationship with her best male friend, Geoff. Publicly they are strictly platonic, impossible to be anything else. Privately, Megan is destructively jealous of anyone interested in Geoff. Megan's public self is wild, almost out of control. To the world, she is the most popular kid at school. Inside, Megan is lost, lonely, and full of self-doubt.

3. **Using computer-mediated communication to manage their relationships seems second-nature to these characters. Identify examples from the film when the characters used technology to manage their lives. Did the use of these technologies help or hinder their relationships? How realistic are the film's examples, from your personal experiences?**

Beyond dyadic face-to-face communication, the film also provides several examples of computer-mediated communication (CMC) and the use of technology. For instance, numerous scenes show at least one student checking messages or texting during class, and other characters texting while having face-to-face conversations. When Lorrin breaks up with Jake, she is more interested in her cell phone screen than making eye contact with him; the cause of their break-up, Lorrin cheating on Jake, also began through texting. And Jake himself would rather play video games and inhabit a virtual world instead of interacting with real people. All of these examples may seem commonplace and ordinary for this age group. Yet, the film shows the ubiquity of technology in young persons' lives, and the continual distractions that often accompany the technology.

One specific theory of CMC, social context cues, argues that technology causes its users to feel less inhibited during interaction. In other words, persons will say and do things via CMC that they would not do face-to-face. One example from the film involves Megan, her best male friend Geoff, and another girl (Erica) who is interested in Geoff. Erica emails Geoff a picture of herself, topless. Megan becomes jealous and in what appears to be a matter of minutes the picture is circulated electronically throughout the entire high school. In the aftermath, we see Erica tearfully explain what happened to her and how she feels. In a shorter, though still painful, example, Mitch breaks up with Hannah via a text message. His choice of medium to terminate the relationship says something about his commitment to Hannah, or at least his immaturity.

4. **The film also provides insight into the characters' relationships with their families. Choose Hannah, Megan, or Colin, and analyze their family system. How is power expressed by the parents and their children? What double-binds do the parents create? What roles do other members play in their family?**

Hannah – Hannah's family has its own set of issues because of her mother's depression and her father's absence. Living with her grandmother, we don't see many interactions between Hannah and her parents. Those few scenes do offer a peek into their family system. In one scene, Hannah's father is there to encourage her to go back to school, even driving her in personally. He performs the role of enabler, however, when he ultimately backs down and allows Hannah to continue to miss school. Hannah's mother, in contrast, demonstrates the one-up position. In another scene, she literally tells Hannah that "you are not special…we've always tried to teach you that." Now Hannah's self-concept makes sense.

Megan – Megan's family provides clear examples of family systems and homeostasis. Megan's older sister was the hero of her family. When she committed suicide that role went vacant, the family was out of balance, and Megan felt the logical force to fill that role. The interaction patterns between Megan and her father are also noteworthy. Megan experiences pressure from her father to attend Notre Dame, his alma mater, and he often places her in a double-bind. For example, in one scene her father tells her not to be "disappointed for me" if she is not accepted. Yet, because the message comes from her father, someone in a powerful position whom Megan admires, that statement is a no-win situation for her. If she is accepted, he will be proud of her because he is her father; if she is not accepted, he will not be disappointed – because he is her father. Clearly Megan can't win.

Colin – Colin's relationship with his father presents additional examples of interaction patterns and double-binds, though Colin's dad uses a different strategy. We witness several scenes making it obvious that Colin looks up to his dad, he has power over Colin. With that in mind, Colin's dad is more subtle exercising his power: he chooses to use humor. In front of Colin's friends, his dad teases him about his grades, the chances of getting a scholarship, and his basketball team. Colin's double-bind occurs before an important basketball game. His dad tells him that his performance tonight will likely determine a college scholarship. But he tells Colin not to worry, it's just another game. His dad also says that without a scholarship, his family cannot afford to send him to college – but again don't worry about it, it's just another game. Given these confusing messages, it's no surprise Colin struggles to play well in the game

.

BABEL

Film Data
Year: 2006
Director: Alejandro González Iñárritu
Length: 143 minutes
Rated: R

Characters/Actors
Richard: Brad Pitt
Susan: Cate Blanchett
Amelia: Adriana Barraza
Santiago: Gael García Bernal
Chieko: Rinko Kikuchi

Communication Concepts
Interpersonal and Impersonal Communication
Needs Met by Communication
Perception and Stereotyping

Viewing Information
     This film may require some preparation to maintain viewer interest. The introductions to the different families, cultures, and locations are slow and seemingly unrelated. From the middle of the movie on, however, illustrations of communication concepts are plentiful. A warning: the film has scenes of graphic nudity, sexual content, drug use, and language

Synopsis
     In the remote Moroccan desert, tragedy strikes when an errant rifle shot seriously injures Susan (Blanchett), as she and her husband Richard (Pitt) confront the misery of their unhappy marriage. This accident starts a chain of events that connect the residents of a North African village, the American couple, their nanny Amelia and her son Santiago (García Bernal), and Chieko (Kikuchi), a rebellious deaf Japanese teenager. As the film's promotional materials proclaim, this complicated story "demonstrates the necessity and importance of human communication."

Discussion Questions
1. What are some examples of problematic communication in the film?

2. How does the film illustrate four types of needs met by communication?

3. Provide examples of impersonal and interpersonal relationships in the film. How do these relationships change over the course of the movie?

BOYZ N THE HOOD

Film Data
Year: 1991
Director: John Singleton
Length: 112 minutes
Rated: R

Characters/Actors
Tre Styles: Cuba Gooding, Jr.
Doughboy: Ice Cube
Ricky Baker: Morris Chestnut
Furious (Fury) Styles: Laurence Fishburne
Brandi: Nia Long
Mrs. Baker: Tyra Ferrell
Reva Styles: Angela Bassett

Communication Concepts
Communication Climate
Conflict
Self-Concept

Viewing Information
This is a powerful movie that offers an important glimpse into a world that is rarely depicted in Hollywood films. The language is rough and the violence is graphic, but so are the streets of South Central Los Angeles. *Boyz* takes place in a black, urban, crime-ridden neighborhood, and involves a stark depiction of family life, illustrating the power of confirming/disconfirming communication.

Synopsis
Boyz N the Hood offers a rare glimpse into the mean streets of (and friendships within) a South Central Los Angeles neighborhood. Tre (Gooding), Doughboy (Ice Cube), and Ricky (Chestnut) become lifelong pals after Tre moves into the neighborhood to live with his father, Furious "Fury" Styles (Fishburne). Ricky and Doughboy, half brothers being raised by a single mother, choose different paths while growing up. Doughboy's life is filled with crime, gang life, and "hangin' out." Ricky is a star football player who pursues a college scholarship as a ticket out of "the hood." Tre is a model of strength and character, due in large part to his father's guidance. Fury disciplines, mentors, and befriends Tre; as a result, Tre has a solid personal and moral foundation.

Although the story is set on a pleasant-looking street, the threat of gangs, drugs, and violence is ever-present (particularly at night, when the streets become a war zone). At several points in the movie, Fury offers compelling arguments about the problems of (and solutions for) their neighborhood and their culture. Ricky, who listens to and respects Tre's dad, nevertheless becomes a victim of a gang shooting. Ricky's murder pushes Tre to the brink; he wants revenge for his best friend's death. Instead, he takes the high road and walks away. The movie's endnotes declare what would be easy to guess: Doughboy becomes another victim of "the hood," while Tre goes on to college.

Discussion Questions
1. Discuss the differences in Tre's, Ricky's, and Doughboy's self-concepts. Explain how they are affected by reflected appraisal and confirming/disconfirming messages.

2. Discuss the reasons for, and approaches to, conflict in "the hood."

THE BREAKFAST CLUB

Film Data
Year: 1985
Director: John Hughes
Length: 92 minutes
Rated: R

Characters/Actors
Andrew Clark: Emilio Estevez
Richard Vernon: Paul Gleason
Brian Johnson: Anthony Michael Hall
Carl: John Kapelos
John Bender: Judd Nelson
Claire Standish: Molly Ringwald
Allison Reynolds: Ally Sheedy

Communication Concepts
Critical Thinking
Group Cohesiveness
Group Development
Perception
Power
Roles
Self-Disclosure
Status

Viewing Information
The movie clearly subscribes to an "ideology of intimacy." The moral of the story appears to be that openness and honesty—even with complete strangers—will make a person happy, healthy, and wise. Something to think about as you watch the film is "Do you think the members of the Breakfast Club will remain friends?" While those who love happy endings may answer yes, many realistically acknowledge that peer pressure from the members' cliques will keep them from interacting on Monday. If this is true, then the five teenagers in the movie have handed intimate, personal, and private information to people who may be their social enemies (or at least competitors) at school. In a worst-case scenario, their self-disclosures could become inter-clique arsenal in the weeks that follow. The pros and cons of self-disclosure are an integral issue in *The Breakfast Club*.

Synopsis
The Breakfast Club takes place at an Illinois high school, where five dissimilar students are sentenced to spend a Saturday detention session together. In attendance is a "princess" (Ringwald), an "athlete" (Estevez), a "brain" (Hall), a "criminal" (Nelson), and a "basket case" (Sheedy). These titles identify the roles the students play during the school week. Because of stereotypes and status levels associated with each role, the students want nothing to do with each other at the outset of the session. However, when confronted by the authoritarian detention teacher (Gleason) and by eight hours of time to kill, the students begin to interact. Through self-disclosure they learn that they are more similar than different. Each wrestles with self-acceptance; each longs for parental approval; each fights against peer pressure. They break through the role barriers and gain greater understanding and acceptance of each other and of themselves. They ultimately develop a group identity and dub themselves "The Breakfast Club."

Discussion Questions
1. How do the characters deviate from their normal roles during the detention session?

2. What is the status of each character prior to the detention session? How does this change during their detention session?

3. What power resources and discussion roles are exhibited in the movie?

4. Discuss the group's developmental stages.

5. What factors contribute to the group's cohesiveness?

6. Discuss the role that perception and stereotyping play in this movie.

THE BREAK-UP

Film Data
Year: 2006
Director: Peyton Reed
Length: 106 minutes
Rated: PG-13

Characters/Actors
Gary Grobowski: Vince Vaughn
Brooke Meyers: Jennifer Aniston
Addie: Joey Lauren Adams
Johnny O: Jon Favreau
Marilyn Dean: Judy Davis
Dennis Grobowski: Vincent D'Onofrio
Lupus Grobowski: Cole Hauser

Communication Concepts
Conflict Management Styles
Content- and Relational-Level Meanings
Language Styles (low- and high-context)
Listening Responses (supportive and non-supportive)
Relational Dialectics (independence-autonomy)
Relational Stages

Viewing Information
Why do women and men struggle to understand each other? And why can it be so difficult to tell our partners how we really feel? This unconventional romantic-comedy attempts to answer these, and other, questions regarding the coming apart stages of interpersonal relationships.

Synopsis
The Break-Up is a unique romantic-comedy. Instead of the usual happily-ever-after plot, the film portrays what can happen when a couple struggles with the end of their relationship. Brooke is an art gallery assistant who wants more than anything else to have Gary want to work on their relationship. Gary is a tour bus guide who wants more than anything else to be left alone. The two are so incompetent in their attempts to repair their relationship it's no wonder they end in a break-up.

Discussion Questions
1. Identify the relational stages and dialectical tensions Gary and Brooke experience, and describe how these lead to their break-up.

2. Describe the supportive and non-supportive messages directed at Gary and Brooke by their friends and family members.

3. Explain how both low- and high-context language styles are present in the film.

4. Identify the styles of conflict used by Brooke and Gary.

BRIDGET JONES'S DIARY

Film Data
Year: 2001
Director: Sharon McGuire
Length: 98 minutes
Rated: R

Characters/Actors
Bridget Jones: Renée Zellweger
Mark Darcy: Colin Firth
Daniel Cleaver: Hugh Grant
Bridget's Mum: Gemma Jones
Bridget's Dad: Jim Broadbent

Communication Concepts
Communication Competence
Self-Concept

Viewing Information
This is a fun film that resonates with young women. Bridget's obsession with her weight, appearance, and clothing will ring true for many college-age females who are bombarded with interpersonal and media messages about thinness, beauty, and apparel. The movie also raises interesting questions about what Bridget wants in a relationship: Does she want a "good man" (Mark) or a "bad boy" (Daniel)? It appears she wants both—and the final lines of the movie suggest that Mark might be able to fill both roles. The movie is rated R for language (liberal use of the "f-word") and sexuality (including a brief nude scene).

Synopsis
Bridget Jones (Zellweger) is a single British woman in her early 30s who worries that she will die "fat and alone." By her own admission she drinks too much, smokes too much, and is overweight—all factors contributing to her fragile self-esteem. Her self-concept and communication competence (or lack thereof) are central features in her relationships with Mark Darcy (Firth) and Daniel Cleaver (Grant), both of whom vacillate between courting and dumping Bridget in a variety of romantic (and humorous) encounters. By the end of the film, Bridget decides which man truly loves her—and that she likes herself "just as she is."

Discussion Questions
1. Describe how Bridget's self-concept is constructed (and deconstructed/reconstructed) through reflected appraisal and social comparison.

2. Describe Bridget's communication competence/incompetence in interpersonal, public speaking, and interviewing situations.

DEAD POETS SOCIETY

Film Data
Year: 1989
Director: Peter Weir
Length: 128 Minutes
Rated: PG

Characters/Actors
John Keating: Robin Williams
Neil Perry: Robert Sean Leonard
Todd Anderson: Ethan Hawke
Knox Overstreet: Josh Charles
Charlie Dalton: Gale Hansen
Richard Cameron: Dylan Kussman
Steven Meeks: Allelon Ruggiero
Gerard Pitts: James Waterston
Mr. Perry: Kurtwood Smith

Communication Concepts
Communication Climate
Conflict
Critical Thinking
Defiance
Group Development
Group Polarization
Self-Concept

Viewing Information
Dead Poets Society is set in an all-male prep school, but the concepts of conformity, authority, and defiance are universal in their appeal and application. This entry touches on only some of the communication topics illustrated in the film. Other issues that can be analyzed include persuasion, ethics, and critical thinking. On the surface, Keating is a "good guy" who gets the students to think for themselves and to stand up for their beliefs. On the other hand, it is worth questioning whether Keating gets the students to think for themselves or whether he merely gets them to think like him. Keating's radical ideas in the hands of impressionable teenagers lead to a variety of negative outcomes, most notably Neil's suicide. Is Keating responsible, at least in part, for Neil's death? Does he appropriately mentor the students he influences? Is it ethical to encourage boys to engage in behaviors that are contrary to the wishes of their parents and the school's administration?

Synopsis
Carpe Diem: Seize the day. This is the lesson John Keating (Williams), an unorthodox teacher at an all-male prep school in New England, wants to convey to his impressionable students. Keating is an alumnus of the school, Welton Academy, and hopes to make his students as curious and iconoclastic as he was (and is). Keating encourages them to "suck the marrow out of life," pursue their dreams, and find their voice. He does so with unusual teaching methods, such as tearing pages from textbooks, kicking soccer balls while shouting poetry, and standing on desks to gain a different perspective. These approaches are frowned upon by the administrators at conservative Welton, whose creed is "Tradition, Honor, Discipline, and Excellence."

Many of the students are captivated by Keating's ideas and ideals. At his prompting, they form a secret club called the Dead Poets Society (DPS), whose primary activity is reading poetry in a cave in the middle of the night. Many of the DPS members experiment with "risky shift" behaviors, due in part to the effect of group polarization. Charlie Dalton (Hansen), an already extroverted student, assumes a new identity as "Nuwanda" and becomes the DPS's daredevil leader. Knox Overstreet (Charles), a quiet student, chases (and ultimately catches) a football player's girlfriend. Todd Anderson (Hawke), a shy boy who is in his brother's shadow at home, gains a sense of acceptance, confidence, and self-worth. Most notably, Neil Perry (Leonard) joins a local theater production and falls in love with acting. This leads to a confrontation with his authoritarian father (Smith). When the conflict seems irresolvable, Neil commits suicide. The school fires Keating, charging that he is responsible for Neil's death because he incited the boys to rebellion. As Keating leaves the school, the boys demonstrate their loyalty to him (and defiance of the administration) by standing on their desks and calling him "Captain."

Discussion Questions

1. Discuss the group development of the Dead Poets Society (DPS).

2. What methods are used by Welton's administration to discourage defiance among the students?

3. Discuss the communication climate and conflict styles in Neil's relationship with his father (Mr. Perry).

4. How does Todd Anderson's self-concept develop over the course of the movie?

THE DEVIL WEARS PRADA

Film Data
Year: 2006
Director: David Frankel
Length: 109 minutes
Rated: PG-13

Characters/Actors
Miranda Priestly: Meryl Streep
Andy Sachs: Anne Hathaway
Nigel: Stanley Tucci

Communication Concepts
Defensive Communication
Listening Behaviors
Organizational Culture
Self-Presentation

Viewing Information

The Oscar-nominated *The Devil Wears Prada* is a fun and enjoyable film. Almost anyone will easily relate to the character of Andy Sachs and be amused by Miranda Priestly's obviously poor interpersonal communication skills. Examples abound in this funny and dramatic 2006 film, making it simple to glean lessons for how to (and how to not) behave in the workplace.

Synopsis

Recent college graduate Andrea Sachs (Hathaway) becomes an assistant to the mercilessly demanding fashion magazine editor Miranda Priestly (Streep). In nearly every interaction between Priestly and Sachs, the self-absorbed boss demonstrates that she values herself more than others and cares little about communicating competently or positively. The workaholic diva harshly criticizes all of her underlings, ignores their contributions, speaks cruelly, dismisses them or leaves the room in mid-sentence. Priestly offers few positive cues (verbal and nonverbal) in exchanges with her colleagues.

Discussion Questions

1. Which of Gibb's defense-provoking behaviors are utilized by Miranda Priestly?

2. Describe Miranda Priestly's listening behaviors.

3. Describe some of the messages about body image and body distortion issues present in the film.

4. What disconfirming messages does Andrea send to her boyfriend and friends once her work at the magazine becomes her major focus?

GRAN TORINO

Film Data
Year: 2008
Director: Clint Eastwood
Length: 116 Minutes
Rated: R

Characters/Actors
Walt Kowalski: Clint Eastwood
Thao: Bee Vang
Sue: Ahney Her
Father Janovich: Christopher Carley
Barber Martin: John Carroll Lynch
Mitch Kowalski: Brian Haley

Communication Concepts
Adapting to Diversity
Linguistic Divergence/Convergence
Speech Codes Theory

Viewing Information
Veteran actor Clint Eastwood directs himself in this story about one man's resistance to changes in his neighborhood, and changes in his life. Not unlike his many past performances as an outlaw cowboy or police officer operating on the fringe, Eastwood's character in *Gran Torino* is a reluctant hero. He has little time or patience for people who are not like him, and he is not shy about expressing his discontent. Through interpersonal communication Eastwood learns to not only tolerate his new neighbors, he gains intercultural understanding as well. In the end, *Gran Torino* provides a moral lesson in both sacrifice and acceptance.

Synopsis
Eastwood plays Walt Kowalski, a retired autoworker and Korean War veteran living out his remaining days at his home. In Walt's world, nothing is supposed to change: children should always respect their elders, a man should be able take care of his own home, and people should live with their own kind. Walt's worldview changes dramatically when he gets to know his Hmong neighbors, and becomes an unwilling mentor for Thao, a young Hmong man in need of direction. Despite his crusty exterior and callous demeanor, Walt becomes both hero and savior for the entire neighborhood.

Discussion Questions
1. Analyze Walt's process of adapting to cultural diversity, including resistance, tolerance, and understanding. Identify differences between Walt's culture and the Hmong people.

2. Looking closely at Walt's communication style, how would you describe his language? What are the meanings and purposes Walt attaches to talk? Finally, contrast Walt's communication style with Thao's and Sue's.

3. Using speech codes theory, analyze Walt's personal and social identity. Identify examples when Walt teaches these speech codes to Thao.

THE GREAT DEBATERS

Film Data
Year: 2007
Director: Denzel Washington
Length: 126 Minutes
Rated: PG-13

Characters/Actors
Melvin B. Tolson: Denzel Washington
Henry Lowe: Nate Parker
Samantha Booke: Jurnee Smollett
James Farmer, Jr.: Denzel Whitaker
Dr. James Farmer, Sr.: Forest Whitaker
Hamilton Burgess: Jermaine Williams
Sheriff Dozier: John Heard

Communication Concepts
Leadership
Persuasive Appeals (Ethos, Pathos, Logos)
Power in Groups
Small Group Cohesiveness
Social Judgment Theory

Viewing Information
Based on the true story of the 1935 Wiley College Debate Team, this film is a dramatic account of confronting intolerance through speech. With eloquent oratory, the film illustrates well how persuasion can be used to change minds, and history. Students should recognize Denzel Washington and Forest Whitaker in their respective roles as debate coach and professor. However, it is the cast of young actors portraying the debate team who deserves consideration.

Synopsis
The Great Debaters is a moving, inspirational story about how the power of speech can overcome prejudice. The film is set in southern Texas in the 1930s, a time and place of racial intolerance, where Jim Crow laws were still on the books and lynchings were a common spectacle. At small, historically-Black Wiley College, students on the debate team not only challenge each other, they confront the prevailing social ideologies head-on. With the help of their charismatic and eloquent coach, real-life poet Melvin B. Tolson, the Wiley College Debate Team gains national recognition as one of the first Black colleges to debate White students. Their prominence culminates with a nationally broadcast debate with Harvard University. In the end the debaters gain more than a simple victory, they gain respect for themselves and their race.

Discussion Questions

1. Identify examples of social judgment theory, including latitudes of acceptance, rejection, and non-commitment. How does ego-involvement influence the persuasive process?

2. How do the debaters utilize appeals to ethos, pathos, and logos in their arguments? Which type of appeal do you find most persuasive? Why?

3. Explain the factors or reasons why the Wiley College Debaters become a cohesive group.

4. Identify examples of power used by the characters. Which types of power are effective? Which types are appropriate?

I'VE LOVED YOU SO LONG

Film Data
Year: 2008
Director: Philippe Claudel
Length: 117 Minutes
Rated: PG-13

Characters/Actors
Juliette: Kristin Scott Thomas
Lea: Elsa Zylberstein
Luc: Serge Hazanavicius
Michel: Laurent Grevill
Capitaine Faure: Frederic Pierrot
Papy Paul: Jean-Claude Arnaud

Communication Concepts
Privacy Management
Self-Disclosure
Uncertainty Reduction

Viewing Information
Don't be fooled by the title. More mystery than romance, the film will keep you guessing until the final climatic scene. Kristin Scott Thomas is one of those actors whom you might have seen before, though perhaps you have difficulty remembering where. (See *Life as a House, The Horse Whisperer,* or *The English Patient*). This is a French-language film, but don't let that deter you. In a performance worthy of her Golden Globe nomination, Scott Thomas delivers a character both nuanced and understated.

Synopsis
Juliette (Scott Thomas) is a lost soul, an empty shell of the person she used to be. Released from prison after serving 15 years for an unspeakable crime, she reluctantly agrees to be taken in by her younger sister's family. Her sister, Lea, desperately wants Juliette back in her life; Lea's husband, Luc, is less accommodating. One might assume that being free again would be a liberating moment, but not for Juliette. She struggles to merge back into society and to keep hidden the secret surrounding her crime. With the persistence of her sister and the empathy of others (Michel and Capitaine Faure), Juliette eventually lets down her guard. Through the process of self-disclosure she reveals her secret and starts to rebuild her relationships with others.

Discussion Questions
1. Apply principles of social penetration to Juliette's relationship with other characters. How do depth, breadth, and reciprocity explain her disclosures? How do conversations and interactions with other characters reduce uncertainty?

2. How does Juliette struggle to reveal, or conceal, her privacy to others? What rules influence how she manages her privacy boundaries? What are the consequences of telling others about her past, versus concealing it?

KNOCKED UP

Film Data
Year: 2007
Director: Judd Apatow
Length: 133 Minutes
Rated: R

Characters/Actors
Ben Stone: Seth Rogen
Alison Scott: Katherine Heigl
Pete: Paul Rudd
Debbie: Leslie Mann

Communication Concepts
Gendered Language
Relational Dialectics Theory
Relationship Stages and Commitment
Uncertainty Reduction Theory

Viewing Information
Knocked Up will never be confused with a storybook romantic-comedy. On the contrary, the appeal of the film is its modern take on dating, commitment, and the responsibilities of adulthood. Rogen's performance as slacker Ben Stone is classic Judd Apatow material, and Heigl as Alison Scott is a breakout role from her *Grey's Anatomy* character on television. Embedded within all the one-liners about sex and drugs, lies a film with a message: Be prepared to change your approach—including your communication—when life throws you a curveball.

Synopsis
Ben Stone is the quintessential slacker: he doesn't have a real job and spends most of his time smoking pot with his like-minded friends. Alison Scott, on the other hand, is the anti-Ben. Smart, attractive, and successful in her work, Alison seems to have the world at her feet. Out on the town celebrating her promotion, Alison meets and has a one-night-stand with Ben. The next day she realizes her mistake and ends their relationship. There's just one minor detail – she later discovers she's pregnant with Ben's child. In an effort to do what's right for their baby, Alison and Ben become a couple. What follows is a comedy about commitment, responsibility, and the realization that life doesn't care about the plans that you make.

Discussion Questions
1. Use uncertainty reduction theory to analyze conversations between Alison and Ben as they get to know each other.

2. Apply Knapp's stages of development and decline to the relationship between Alison and Ben.

3. Which relational dialectics are Debbie and Pete experiencing? How are they choosing to manage their dialectics?

4. What gendered language differences are present in the conversations among Alison, Ben, Debbie, and Pete?

LARS AND THE REAL GIRL

Film Data
Year: 2007
Director: Craig Gillespie
Length: 106 Minutes
Rated: PG-13

Characters/Actors
Lars: Ryan Gosling
Karin: Emily Mortimer
Gus: Paul Schneider
Dr. Dagmar: Patricia Clarkson
Margo: Kelli Garner

Communication Concepts
Coordinated Management of Meaning Theory
Relational Dialectics
Relationship Stages
Symbolic Interactionism Theory

Viewing Information
If you only read the DVD jacket of *Lars and the Real Girl*, you might conclude that the plot is hard to believe. On the contrary, this critically-acclaimed film provides touching moments of community support and interpersonal understanding. Gosling gives a memorable performance as Lars, a delusional man searching for intimacy.

Synopsis
Lars Lindstrom is a shy, sweet man who lives by himself in his brother's garage. When Lars brings his new girlfriend (Bianca) home to meet his brother (Gus) and sister-in-law (Karin), they are thrilled – until they learn that she is an anatomically correct mannequin. At the urging of their family doctor, Gus and Karin go along with Lars' delusion. Eventually, the whole town treats Lars and Bianca as if their relationship is real. The film shows how an entire community can come together to support one individual, and how communication works to create our reality.

Discussion Questions
1. Do Lars and Bianca have a "real" interpersonal relationship?

2. Apply Knapp's stages of development and decline to the relationship between Lars and Bianca.

3. Using symbolic interactionism theory (meaning, language, and thought), describe how the characters co-construct their reality through communication. How does the community of townspeople, the generalized other, contribute to the film's narrative?

4. Apply CMM theory to the film by explaining the regulative and constitutive rules the characters follow, including both coordinated and uncoordinated meanings.

THE LAST KISS

Film Data
Year: 2006
Director: Tony Goldwyn
Length: 104 Minutes
Rated: R

Characters/Actors
Michael: Zach Braff
Jenna: Jacinda Barrett
Kim: Rachel Bilson
Chris: Casey Affleck
Izzy: Michael Weston
Kenny: Eric Christian Olsen
Anna: Blythe Danner
Stephen: Tom Wilkinson

Communication Concepts
Deception
Relational Dialectics
Self-Disclosure and Emotional Expression

Viewing Information

The Last Kiss, marketed as a "contemporary" romantic-comedy, follows a somewhat unconventional plot. A remake of the 2001 Italian film *L'ultimo bacio*, it explores a "darker side" of deception and infidelity. It is a story about dysfunction, the consequences of the decisions people make within their relationships, and the costs of forgiveness.

Synopsis

Michael (Braff) seems to have it all: a beautiful girlfriend (Barrett) who clearly loves him, a stable career as an architect, and the closeness that only a group of long-term friends can provide. Indeed, he has everything he ever dreamed for – and that is his dilemma. When Jenna announces that she is pregnant and starts talking about marriage and buying a house, Michael wonders if life as he knows it is now over. He begins to question his commitment to Jenna. That commitment is tested when Michael meets Kim (Bilson) at the wedding of a mutual friend. Kim's free-spirited persona and attractive appearance tempt Michael, and he ends up cheating on Jenna. What results is a series of lies perpetuated by Michael, Jenna's discovery of these lies and his infidelity, and Michael's attempts to repair their relationship.

Incidentally, Michael and Jenna are not the only characters in the film suffering from relational discord. Michael's friend Izzy (Weston) can't seem to let go of a past relationship, driving him to near depression. Another friend, Chris (Affleck), constantly argues with his neurotic wife about taking care of their newborn child, prompting him to suggest that they split up. And Jenna's parents, Anna (Danner) and Stephen (Wilkinson), are going through their own discovery of infidelity after thirty years of marriage.

Discussion Questions

1. Describe the dialectical tensions Michael is experiencing in his relationship with Jenna, and how he chooses to manage those tensions.

2. How do Michael and Jenna talk about their relational expectancies through self-disclosure and emotional expression?

3. What verbal and nonverbal cues give Michael away when he lies to Chris? What cues give Chris away when he lies to Jenna? How does Jenna's suspicion affect the outcome?

4. What are the consequences of deception presented in the film?

LITTLE MISS SUNSHINE

Film Data
Year: 2006
Directors: Valerie Faris, Jonathan Dayton
Length: 101 minutes
Rated: R

Characters/Actors
Olive: Abigail Breslin
Richard: Greg Kinnear
Grandpa: Alan Arkin
Sheryl: Toni Collette
Frank: Steve Carell
Dwayne: Paul Dano

Communication Concepts
Confirming/Disconfirming Communication
Family Communication
Self-Concept Formation
Self-Disclosure

Viewing Information
This heart-warming, popular film first strikes most viewers with the sheer dysfunction of its family members; but the hilarity of the situations coupled with the personal growth of its characters increases its applicability to interpersonal communication concepts. There is some sexual and drug content.

Synopsis
Little Miss Sunshine chronicles the adventures of 7-year-old Olive (Breslin) and her dysfunctional family as they travel from New Mexico to California, where Olive is to compete in the Little Miss Sunshine beauty contest. Olive's relatives are so burdened with their own quirks and neuroses that making it to California sane, alive and on time for the pageant is uncertain until the end of the film. From tensions revealed early in the movie (i.e., the explosive dinner scene), it's clear that the 800-mile journey could do irreparable harm to each family member, and to all of their strained relationships. Along the way, the Hoover family members experience profound changes, individually and collectively, as they all begin to share closely held personal secrets and experiences — and in so doing grow closer.

Discussion Questions
1. Describe the disconfirming messages presented by the various characters in the film.

2. Describe the confirming messages presented by Sheryl in the film.

3. Describe how the characters disclose personal information throughout the trip and how that disclosure enhances their relationships.

4. How did the family members bond and find a sense of cohesiveness in the 800-mile journey?

5. Describe Olive's self-concept and body image.

OFFICE SPACE

Film Data
Year: 1999
Director: Mike Judge
Length: 88 minutes
Rated: R

Characters/Actors
Peter Gibbons: Ron Livingston
Joanna: Jennifer Aniston
Milton: Stephen Root
Samir: Ajay Naidu
Michael Bolton: David Herman
Bill Lumbergh: Gary Cole

Communication Concepts
Communication Climate
Classical Theory/Theory X
Conflict
Honesty/Lying
Language
Self-Concept/Identity Management

Viewing Information
The back cover of the *Office Space* video proudly announces that the film is by Mike Judge, creator of *Beavis and Butt-head*, which should serve warning that the movie has some crude content and language (as well as two brief sexual scenes). While this is a very humorous film, it touches on some serious issues that can be explored. (For example, see "Investigating the Relationship Between Superior-Subordinate Relationship Quality and Employee Dissent" by J. W. Kassing in *Communication Research Reports* (2000), Vol. 17, pp. 58–69).

One of the unstated morals of *Office Space* is that Peter's life becomes better when he stops closely managing his identity and begins doing and saying whatever he wants. While this makes for an entertaining movie (and is the premise for other entertaining films such as *Liar Liar*), the outcomes of Peter's decisions can and should be a point of discussion for communication students. Would Peter actually be promoted to management if he ignored his boss, came to work whenever he wanted, dressed in shorts, destroyed company property, and admitted his lack of motivation to outside consultants? Probably only in Hollywood, which makes this a good case study for debating the pros and cons of identity management, honesty, and rhetorical sensitivity in the workplace.

Synopsis
Peter Gibbons (Livingston) and his colleagues Samir (Naidu) and Michael (Herman) are computer specialists who are fed up with their mundane jobs. They work at Initech Corporation, an impersonal organization with a Classical Theory/Theory X approach to management. Their boss Lumbergh (Cole) has a condescending attitude and creates a defensive communication climate with all employees, including Milton (Root), the emotionally challenged mailroom clerk who keeps threatening to "burn the building." In a hypnotherapy session, Peter loses his inhibitions and starts speaking his mind around the office. His "straight shooting" earns him a promotion while others are downsized out of the company. Peter and his colleagues carry out a high-tech embezzling scheme to get revenge on Initech. Peter's new girlfriend Joanna (Aniston) is also fed up with her waitress job and her manager; however, she helps Peter realize that embezzling is an unethical way to handle his frustration with Initech. Ultimately, Peter and his friends move on to new horizons and Initech (quite literally) goes up in flames.

Discussion Questions

1. Describe how the Initech Corporation illustrates Classical Theory and Theory X approaches to organizational communication.

2. Describe the communication climate in manager-employee interactions in the movie.

3. What styles of conflict management are used by the managers and employees in the movie?

4. Describe the changes Peter experiences in his identity management.

OUTSOURCED

Film Data
Year: 2006
Director: John Jeffcoat
Length: 103 Minutes
Rated: PG-13

Characters/Actors
Todd Anderson: Josh Hamilton
Asha: Ayesha Dharker
Puro: Asif Basra
Dave: Matt Smith

Communication Concepts
Adapting to Diversity
Culture Shock
Individualism and Collectivism
Organizational Culture
Proxemics

Viewing Information
A light-hearted comedy with a likable cast, *Outsourced* provides examples of contemporary business practices in the same way *Office Space* put the spotlight on the cubicle culture. Part cross-cultural sojourn and part international business, the film attempts to capture what happens when your job, and everyone who works for you, is outsourced to India. Hamilton portrays the business everyman, Dharker is his opinionated love interest, and Basra is Todd's charming and energetic replacement.

Synopsis
So far, the life of Todd Anderson has been predictable and uneventful. He manages a customer service call center in Seattle, for a company selling novelty products. However, his world is turned upside down when his job, and everyone under him, is outsourced to India. If being fired weren't bad enough, Todd's boss strong-arms him into going to India to train his replacement. In India Todd is overwhelmed by the cultural differences, both in and out of the new call center. He eventually finds a way to train his new staff and increase their productivity, but not before Todd learns something about himself.

Discussion Questions
1. Identify examples of Todd's culture shock, including his loss of personal space. Also, apply Edward Hall's distances in your explanation.

2. Recognize examples of Todd's individualism and the host culture's collectivism.

3. Provide examples that illustrate Todd's process of adapting to cultural diversity (i.e., resistance, tolerance, understanding, respect, and participation).

4. Analyze the organizational culture of the call center when Todd first arrives compared to the end of the film, including their rituals and customs. How was Todd able to motivate the employees and change their organizational culture?

THE PAINTED VEIL

Film Data
Year: 2006
Director: John Curran
Length: 125 minutes
Rated: PG-13

Characters/Actors
Kitty Fane: Naomi Watts
Walter Fane: Edward Norton
Charlie Townsend: Liev Schreiber

Concepts Illustrated
Confirming/Disconfirming Communication
Dialectical Tensions
Relational Stages

Viewing Information
The Painted Veil may be slow-moving at first, and some may be put off that it's a period piece set primarily in China. However, the development of characters and examples of effective and ineffective interpersonal communication make this film worth the investment of time and energy.

Synopsis
The Painted Veil chronicles the tragic 1920s relationship of a young English couple. Shy bacteriologist Walter Fane (Norton) and vivacious, spirited socialite Kitty (Watts) marry after an all-too-brief courtship, and soon move to Shanghai where Walter pursues his career. Consumed by his work and socially awkward, Walter rarely listens to Kitty's words—and more importantly, to the feelings behind them. Kitty soon finds herself in an affair with witty diplomat Charlie Townsend until husband Walter learns of the infidelity and vengefully forces her to travel with him to help save a war-torn village ravaged by cholera. Their cold, loveless marriage is tested in this remote and dangerous environment, and they begin to heal their relationship through listening and mutual respect.

Discussion Questions
1. Describe the disconfirming messages Walter sends to Kitty.

2. Describe how the relational stages in the couple's relationship.

3. What relational dialectics can be seen in the couple's relationship?

SAY ANYTHING...

Film Data
Year: 1989
Director: Cameron Crowe
Length: 100 minutes
Rated: PG-13

Characters/Actors
Lloyd Dobler: John Cusack
Diane Court: Ione Skye
James Court: John Mahoney
Corey Flood: Lili Taylor
D.C.: Amy Brooks
Rebecca: Pamela Segall

Communication Concepts
Honesty/Lying
Relational Stages
Self-Disclosure

Viewing Information

This is a light, romantic comedy with a serious message about the impact of dishonesty in primary interpersonal relationships. The movie is appropriate for high school or college students (Diane and Lloyd's non-depicted sexual activity might be a sensitive issue for some audiences).

Synopsis

This is a lighthearted tale about an unlikely couple. Lloyd Dobler (Cusack) is unsure what he will do after graduating from high school, except perhaps to pursue his dreams of becoming a professional kick-boxer. Diane Court (Skye) is valedictorian of her class and has plans for college—but unlike Lloyd, she has no social life. They attend a graduation party together, and Diane is pleasantly surprised at how comfortable and happy she feels around Lloyd. Their interest in each other grows and they date throughout the summer.

Diane's parents are divorced and she lives with her father (Mahoney), with whom she has always had open and honest communication. As Diane and Lloyd's relationship develops, Diane's relationship with her father begins to change. Diane's father believes Lloyd is complicating her life and he recommends that she break off her relationship with Lloyd before it becomes too serious. She acquiesces to her father's wishes. Neither Diane nor Lloyd is happy about the breakup, but she keeps telling herself it is for the best.

Diane and her father appear to have a healthy and positive relationship, but when she learns that he has engaged in illegal financial dealings involving the nursing home he runs, her trust in him is shattered. Diane realizes she wants and needs Lloyd and reaches out to him; he supports her while she deals with the devastating fact that her father is not the man she thought he was. Diane tries to reconstruct her relationship with her father before she and Lloyd fly off to England together.

Discussion Questions

   1. What relational stages do Lloyd and Diane experience?

   2. What were some of the reasons for self-disclosure between Diane and her father and between Lloyd and his female friends?

   3. Why did Diane's father choose to lie to her about his finances? What effect did his dishonesty have on Diane and their relationship?

SHOPGIRL

Film Data
Year: 2005
Director: Anand Tucker
Length: 100 Minutes
Rated: R

Characters/Actors
Mirabelle: Claire Danes
Ray Porter: Steve Martin
Jeremy: Jason Schwartzman

Communication Concepts
Dimensions of Intimacy
Relational Dialectics
Stages of Relational Development
Uncertainty Reduction and Social Exchange Theories

Viewing Information
No one will mistake this film for a fast-paced action adventure. Nonetheless, it's easy to identify with the lead character's quest for a satisfying romantic relationship. The moral dilemmas illustrated here aren't easily dismissed. They force us to consider what compromises may be necessary to create a satisfying and fulfilling life.

Synopsis
This bittersweet film follows the romantic adventures of twenty-something Mirabelle Buttersfield (Danes). By day she sells gloves at Saks Fifth Avenue in Beverly Hills; by night she is an aspiring artist. In her search for love, Mirabelle meets two men who couldn't be more different. Jeremy (Schwartzman) is her contemporary. He is loveable, scruffy, funny, poor, and socially inept. Mirabelle's other romantic interest is Ray Porter (Martin), a suave millionaire who is old enough to be her father. Ray showers Mirabelle with gifts, and in short order they become lovers. From the beginning, Ray makes it clear that he is not interested in a long-term commitment, and Mirabelle agrees. But in time she realizes that this arrangement does not fulfill her emotional needs. By movie's end Mirabelle faces the dilemma of whether to continue in a comfortable but unfulfilling relationship with Ray, or to walk away and either choose Jeremy or risk being alone.

Discussion Questions
1. Describe the relational stages in Mirabelle's relationships.

2. Use Social Exchange theory to describe Mirabelle's relationship with Ray.

3. What dimensions of intimacy operate in Mirabelle and Ray's relationship?

4. What dialectical tensions operate in Mirabelle's relationship with Ray?

5. What issues of honesty and clarity arise in the film?

SPANGLISH

Film Data
Year: 2004
Director: James L. Brooks
Length: 131 Minutes
Rated: PG-13

Characters/Actors
John Clasky: Adam Sadler
Deborah Clasky: Téa Leoni
Flor Moreno: Paz Vega
Evelyn Wright: Cloris Leachman
Cristina Moreno: Shelbie Bruce
Bernie Clasky: Sarah Steele
Georgie Clasky: Ian Hyland

Communication Concepts
Control and Power in Relationships
Defensive and Supportive Behaviors
Intercultural Communication
Relational Dialectics
Self-Concept and Identity Management

Viewing Information
This drama-comedy profiles a family with quite different spouses. John Clasky is a devoted and thoughtful father. John's wife Deborah is divisive and condescending. When the radiant Spanish-speaking Flor takes the job of family housekeeper, what follows is a lesson not only in intercultural communication but family values as well.

Synopsis
Spanglish opens with a scene at the Admissions office of Princeton University. In a voice-over, we learn that applicant Cristina Moreno identifies "the most influential person in her life" as her mother – Flor Moreno. What unfolds is a story about Flor's decision to work for an Anglo family, the Claskys, and how her choice changes their lives forever.

The Clasky family consists of father John, mother Deborah, their two children Bernie and Georgie, and Deborah's mother Evelyn Wright. Flor quickly discovers that John is a highly successful, and perhaps overly-emotional, chef; Deborah is neurotic and hyper-competitive, lifting herself up by putting others down; Evelyn is an alcoholic, though kind and generous; and the children are desperate for the positive influence missing from their mother. When Flor and Cristina are forced to move in with the Claskys during the summer, Flor loses all sense of privacy and is on the verge of quitting the job. By film's end, it's up to Flor to make decisions that at least provide a chance of the Claskys rebuilding their lives.

Discussion Questions
1. Identify and contrast examples of Gibb's categories for defensive and supportive behaviors displayed by the characters. What effects do these behaviors have on their relationships?

2. Identify examples of one-up and one-down messages? Which relationships are complementary? Which are symmetrical?

3. Which dialectical tensions do John and Flor experience, both with each other and independently? How do they choose to manage these tensions?

4. How do the characters influence each other's self-concept? What influence does culture have on this process?

UP IN THE AIR

Film Data

Year: 2009
Director: Jason Reitman
Length: 108 Minutes
Rated: R

Characters/Actors

Ryan Bingham: George Clooney
Alex Goran: Vera Farmiga
Natalie Keener: Anna Kendrick
Craig Gregory: Jason Bateman
Bob: J.K. Simmons
Jim Miller: Danny McBride

Communication Concepts

Computer-Mediated Communication
Perspective Taking and Person-Centered Messages
Relational Commitment/Dialectics

Viewing Information

Ryan Bingham is a corporate downsizer who flies around the country firing people and avoiding relationships. Enter Natalie Keener, a feisty college graduate who wants to upend Ryan's business, and Alex Goran, an attractive business traveler who captures Ryan's heart. The results are a funny, ironic take on both romantic relationships and corporate culture. And as the title suggests, both women may indeed leave Ryan "up in the air."

Synopsis

Ryan Bingham is an island surrounded by a sea of travelers. Working for a company that specializes in corporate downsizing, Ryan is paid, essentially, to fire people. And apparently he is very good at what he does: Ryan's company flies him around the country over 300 days out of the year. He also gives motivational speeches about "relational downsizing," and living one's life out of a backpack – a metaphor for Ryan's lifestyle. Clearly more at home on the road, Ryan's way of life is threatened when the company hires Natalie Keener, an overly ambitious college graduate who wants to revolutionize his business: Natalie believes firing employees can be done through teleconferencing and not in person. If that weren't threatening enough, Ryan begins a romantic relationship with fellow business traveler Alex, who causes him to question his self-imposed isolationism. Ryan Bingham might be an island, but he soon realizes that he is not alone.

Discussion Questions

1. Compare and contrast Natalie, Alex, and Ryan, and their divergent views on relational commitment. How does each character define their romantic relationships? How do they manage the autonomy versus connection relational dialectic?

2. Analyze examples of person-centered messages Ryan creates as part of his job, and compare those with the messages he creates while not working. In which context is he more skilled at perspective taking? In which context is he more scripted?

3. Identify examples of computer-mediated communication (CMC) used throughout the film. In the business context, how effective is CMC? How do the characters use CMC outside of work?

WAITRESS

Film Data
Year: 2007
Director: Adrienne Shelly
Length: 104 Minutes
Rating: PG-13

Characters/Actors
Jenna: Keri Russell
Earl: Jeremy Sisto
Dr. Pomatter: Nathan Fillion
Becky: Cheryl Hines
Dawn: Adrienne Shelly
Old Joe: Andy Griffith

Communication Concepts
Confirmation/Disconfirmation
Relational Stages
Social Exchange Theory

Viewing Information
It would be easy to dismiss this film as just another "chick flick," but not so fast – this quirky romantic-comedy provides many relevant examples of relational development and maintenance, along with the unexpected twists life often takes when we're searching for a satisfying romantic relationship.

Synopsis
Jenna (Russell) waits tables at a local diner somewhere in the American South, specializing in unique pies that she creates in her head. The pie names and ingredients typically reflect critical moments in Jenna's life, such as "Falling-in-Love Pie." Unfortunately, Jenna is also trapped in a marriage to a controlling and abusive husband named Earl (Sisto). Her plans to leave her husband are complicated when she learns she's pregnant with Earl's child, and when she begins an affair with the town doctor (Dr. Pomatter, played by Fillion). Through the process of composing letters to her unborn child, and through the support she receives from Dr. Pomatter and her coworkers, Jenna gains enough strength to break free of Earl and "start fresh."

Discussion Questions
1. Provide examples of disconfirming messages Earl uses toward Jenna. How do these messages contribute to the climate of their marriage?

2. Contrast Earl's disconfirming style with Dr. Pomatter's confirming messages.

3. Use Social Exchange theory to explain Jenna's reasons for staying with Earl as long as she did, along with her ultimate decision to leave him.

4. Describe how other characters in the film weigh the costs and rewards of their relationships.

5. Describe the relational stages of Jenna's relationship with Dr. Pomatter.

WHEN HARRY MET SALLY. . .

Film Data
Year: 1989
Director: Rob Reiner
Length: 96 minutes
Rated: R

Characters/Actors
Harry Burns: Billy Crystal
Sally Albright: Meg Ryan
Marie: Carrie Fisher
Jess: Bruno Kirby

Communication Concepts
Gender
Relational Stages

Viewing Information
This is a sweet, funny, and perceptive film that is well known to (and loved by) most college students. The now-famous "orgasm scene" and occasional rough language may make viewing uncomfortable for some, but most are familiar enough with the film that it doesn't faze them. This film is an ideal way to study relational stages. *When Harry Met Sally...* is also a useful tool for discussing topics such as communication climate (which slowly changes from chilly to warm), conflict, and perception.

Synopsis
Harry Burns (Crystal) and Sally Albright (Ryan) are virtual strangers who get together for purely functional reasons: A cross-country car ride in which they share gas costs and driving. She quickly sizes him up as crude and insensitive; he appraises her as naive and obsessive. By the time they finish their journey, they are glad to part ways. However, they continue bumping into each other in the years that follow. Slowly but surely, a friendship develops between them—something that Harry declared could never happen because "men and women can't be friends; the sex thing always gets in the way." Harry and Sally try to set each other up with their friends Jess (Kirby) and Marie (Fisher), but Jess and Marie fall for each other instead. Harry and Sally try dating other people, but clearly they care deeply for each other. Ultimately, their friendship turns into love—but not without some sharp disagreements (and a short breakup) over the role that sex plays in male–female relationships. Their breakup ends when they realize how much they both like and love each other. They marry and (presumably) live happily ever after.

Discussion Questions
1. What gender differences are evident in Harry and Sally's communication?

2. How does (or doesn't) Harry and Sally's relationship match Knapp's model of relational stages?

SECTION III
FEATURE FILM WEBSITES OF INTEREST

Now Playing Online
www.oup.com/us/playingnow

Film Clips Online
www.filmclipsonline.com

Teach with Movies
www.teachwithmovies.org

Hartwick Classic Film Leadership Cases
http://www.hartwickinstitute.org/Store.aspx?Action=Sort&Type=Film

The Internet Movie Database
www.imdb.com

Film.Com
www.film.com

Movie Review Query Engine
www.mrqe.com

Roger Ebert Reviews
rogerebert.suntimes.com

INDEX BY COMMUNICATION CONCEPTS

NOTES

NOTES

NOTES

NOTES

NOTES

NOTES

NOTES

NOTES

NOTES